Grasp

Poems, Prose, and Essays

David Yuen

Special Thanks

To my mom and dad who, through bad times, still loved me more than I deserve.

Special shout out to my brother, Tom.

To Steve, the pastor, friend, and brother who encouraged me to be passionate.

To Clement, Jon G., Jimmy, and Henry for being the guys who kept me accountable in more ways than one.

To my other brothers not in blood but in spirit: Micah, Eric, Ryan, Tyler, Austin, Jon W., Pat, and Kevin.

To Austin Tam who provided his photography for the cover and "A Study of Light and Darkness."

To Grace, a fellow writer, who encouraged my writing with her honest input.

To the rest of my Christian fellowship who has always been a family to me.

To God, who gave me the greatest gift of all:

His Son. Soli Deo gloria

Table of Contents

Men go abroad to wonder at the heights of mountains, at the huge waves of the sea, at the long courses of the rivers, at the vast compass of the ocean, at the circular motions of the stars, and they pass by themselves without wondering.

Saint Augustine

Preface

What is the human condition? It's a very simple, but often over asked question. But nothing is more relevant to ourselves than thinking about the complexity of our own existence. Throughout my time writing this book, the world was still reeling from a global pandemic, political tensions and conflicts were ongoing, and the general sentiment was that of uncertainty. But as the year passed there were still times of hope, times of beauty, times of faith, even in the eye of the many storms that swept the world. In fact, throughout the process of writing the short story, "Grasp", a semi-autobiographical account of a visit to Iceland, the issue of the human struggle took center stage. This along with other things led me to think about what that struggle was.

So if I were to ask myself the question, "what is the human condition?" I would first say that it's many things. It is suffering. It is joy. It is in relationships. It is in the connections we have between ourselves and things that are higher than us. It is an existence filled with wickedness and cruelty, but with moments of goodness and charity. It is something that each of us cannot fully grasp, but at the same time we grasp it every single day. And in the madness of how bad things can get, being human can be at times beautiful.

Our lives are littered with irony because as much as it can be filled with darkness, it can be filled with light. Just as the people we love can hurt us the most, it is because we love them that the wrongs they do to us are amplified. But in forgiving them and loving them, despite these wrongs, can we find the greatest things in the world from the simplest acts. Our humanity is more sophisticated than it seems when we realize what we take for granted. When seen in the correct light, humanity can be the evidence of what is transcendent.

We are creatures of relationships. We are complicated contradictions. We are hated and we are loved. But as imperfect as we are, we are all one important thing: human.

Grasp

It was 12:35 p.m. by the time the tour guide ended the city tour at a local pub where we would try out the typical Reykjavik cuisine. It was a sample course in which you had the option of choosing two out of three dishes. There was a lamb soup, a shellfish soup served in a bread bowl, and another Icelandic fish dish. I chose the first two dishes, and believe me when I say that the lamb soup was nothing to write home about. Honestly, it was all about that shellfish soup.

There was a young couple from Austria with us who couldn't have been older than in their late 20s. Then there was another young couple from Wales, both teachers, and as we sat there drinking in the atmosphere, I could feel the IPA ale flooding my mind and loosening my tongue. We got to talking about Brexit, which had been voted on not too long ago, and how they were worried about it. Wales was going to get hit hard because it was one of the poorer regions of the UK, so if Britain left the EU, things could change for the worse there. It was interesting because in another tour group I was in that week, I met another young Brit, a single mother who was a professional midwife, who was in favor of it. She was from London, and I would imagine things could be different there.

This was my second trip to Iceland. For some reason, I just needed to come back, and I thought 2019 would be a good year to do so. I just felt this strange draw to come back. For a Yank from the States, you would figure that the draws would be obvious: a remote place unlike anything else, an island of ice and fire, the Northern Lights, the whole exotic feeling of it. But the landscape,

1

which sometimes felt like a moonscape at certain points outside the city, made my mind wander. And I'm not sure in what way.

As we talked and commented on the dishes, the tour guide, who had joined us, began commenting on a new line of conversation passing through the group: how Iceland was considered one of the happiest countries in the world, but how it also had a high suicide rate.

At first, people commented that it was probably because of the long dark winters here, but surprisingly, the guide said that people killed themselves most often in the spring and not in the winter. According to him, when people got depressed during the Icelandic winters, they would expect that when the spring came, their mood would improve. But once the sunlight came back and they realized that their mood hadn't really improved, this supposedly drove them to the act.

I then added that this reminded me of what I heard on my trip to Japan a while back, which was that despite how everything is so beautiful and so well done in Japan, the suicide rate there is also high. In fact, in Japan, supposedly, in tall buildings above a certain floor, the windows would be locked to prevent people from opening them to jump out.

The dilemma that we ended up with was how a country could be so seemingly happy on the one hand but so miserable on the other and have both those things be true at once. Some members of our tour, one of them being an elderly woman from Germany, mentioned that the scales they used to measure a country's happiness were independent from the suicide rate, which made sense given that Iceland fit both extremes.

2

I would imagine that the happiness scale had much to do with the benefits and social support the government gave its people, but I wasn't an expert, and I figured that it was better left at that. I gulped down the last of the Icelandic IPA, allowing its subtle sweetness and hoppy bitterness to penetrate through the fog of my contemplation.

Half aware and half "loosened," we were at the end of the meal, which concluded the city tour. I politely pardoned myself from the pub. Though the guide told us that visitors didn't need to tip, he also mentioned that hospitality workers will still happily accept your tip anyway. I decided to be very American and gave him a tip before thanking him. Needless to say, he accepted it with a happy smile as I went outside.

* * *

To wait out my buzz, I found myself standing in front of the Hallgrímskirkja church as various pedestrians and tourists wandered around it, admiring its towering height. It was in the later afternoon that I chose to come here just to clear my head.

Throughout this past week, I had traveled around the island with a small tour group, looking at its geysers, its black sand beaches, its waterfalls, and other sites. And as much as these moments were exhilarating, later on in the trip, I felt a certain melancholy.

I remembered that as our tour bus was traveling to a nearby destination lodge, we had stopped by a scenic spot filled with tiny rock piles that stood out like mini-towers in the landscape. According to our guide, they were called "cairns." In the old days, people built these as navigational markers to help travelers on their journey. In modern times, they could be used by hikers for guidance.

I remembered that when we came out of the tour bus to look at this site, it felt like there were well over a hundred of these markers, all grouped into one location. As I looked out onto that sea of cairns, it felt like one of those Neolithic civilization sites that nameless ancestors had left. Mattie, that midwife from London, eagerly ran out and built her own cairn with unrestrained giddiness. I personally chose not to do that because the more I stared at those cairns, the more they reminded of something else: grave markers.

* * *

Apparently, a majority of the interior of Iceland is uninhabited because of the geothermic and seismic activity at the center of the island. Because of that, nearly the entire population lives on the edge of the island. The interior is also desolate.

One day, our group visited Diamond Beach, a beach littered with large chunks of broken ice. It felt like I was walking through an ice sculpture garden with all types of ice in various shapes and colors. Some of the ice chunks were a rich sky blue, others were white, others were transparent (hence the name of the beach), and still others were dark gray to black.

Thinking that some of the holes and chambers in these chunks of ice would be the freshest water anyone could ever taste, I did a really idiotic thing by scooping up some of it and drinking it. It was all salt water. Spitting it out hilariously in a spray, I felt like kicking myself. And though I didn't, I knew my taste buds were doing a fine job of that for me.

The experience was beautiful, funny, and bittersweet. And now, looking back, here in a square in front of Iceland's most beautiful church, I was amazed at how one moment a person could be having the time of their life and then at the next either be shocked, sad, bored, or upset sometimes without obvious reason.

It was the human dilemma. And, in the end, would any of it matter when our time came and our moments on earth vanished? I felt like kicking myself for suddenly thinking that as I watched an Asian couple take pictures in front of the church. The young girl posed photogenically in front of the chapel, her fingers pushed up against her smiling face in a peace sign, as her boyfriend (I assumed as much) in highlighted hair took an angled shot.

Existentialism is supposedly part of the postmodern movement that advocates that existence does not have any inherent meaning, but rather that meaning is something that an individual must construct for themselves.

In Japan, there's a phenomenon called "Karoshi," in which a person literally works himself to death because of a demanding job situation and Japan's work ethic. Were those people pursuing their meaning? Even to death?

Why did I come back here when I had seen this church and walked these streets already? Just to do it all again?

Apparently, on this trip, I found out that Icelandic is the closest language to Old Norse, much more than any of the other Scandinavian countries, due to the nation's isolation from the world. Also, it's not unusual for people of the same immediate biological family to have different last names because most Icelanders still practice the tradition of using their parent's first name (most of the time their father's) followed by "son" (son of) or "dottir" (daughter of) for their last name, depending on your gender. So if my dad's name was Jon, my last name would have been Jonson, even if his last name was different. If I had a sister, her last name would be Jondottir. Wild, isn't it?

According to Norse mythology, if you died courageously in battle, you would be taken to Valhalla to feast with the gods until Ragnarök came, which was their doomsday. I read somewhere that certain Norsemen, if they didn't die in battle, would purposely cut themselves with their weapons, hoping to fool the gods into believing that they died in battle.

When Ragnarök came, the gods and all of the slain in Valhalla would fight in a war that would lead to the end of existence. Tyr and a wolf named Garm would slay each other. Thor would fight with Jormungand, the large serpent, and that would end them both. In the end, the world would sink into the ocean, and nothing would be left. When that happened, it would be as though the world had never come into being.

* * *

A fog had rolled in by the time we got to the Black Sands Beach. It was a strange, otherworldly experience. This volcanic beach of black sand was lined nearby with cliffs of gray geometric basalt columns.

The pitch-black sand, combined with the echoing crashes of the waves, made me feel as though I was walking through a spirit realm or an afterlife.

I couldn't help but drift in meditation as I, along with other members of my tour group, walked those black shores. As you went closer to the ocean, the black sands turned from large smooth rocks to small pebbles and then slowly into fine onyx silt. I remember at one point reaching down without thinking and scooping up a handful of that sand. I grasped it in my hands before lowering it to allow the incoming wave to draw it out between my loosely clenched fingers. I wasn't sure if I was trying to fight the wave to keep as much of the sand as possible or if I was purposely allowing the ocean to sift the sands between my fingers as though to take relief from the sensation of fullness slowly turning into emptiness.

Dante's *Divine Comedy* portrays Purgatory as a mountain located somewhere in the Southern Hemisphere. Supposedly, as a person ascends each level of the mountain, they go through certain levels of suffering to be purified before entering the presence of God. I'm guessing that Dante chose the Southern Hemisphere simply because it was less known. But I wouldn't know.

It was about three years ago when I brought one of my team members into my office. We had to lay him off because of performance issues, and I had agreed with my HR director to be there when we announced that to him. He was a young man, no older than his late twenties at the time.

When we called him in and sat him down, the HR director, Amy, broke the news to him. I figured that since

7

I was the one who hired him, I should at least be there when the time came to cut him loose.

At first, he was shocked and began promising us that he'd do whatever it takes to make up for things; come in on weekends, or come in early to do extra work. But once we explained to him that it was too late, he told us that he had been contemplating suicide for the past few months and that he had been on certain medications. A moan of stress came out from Amy as we heard the news, which matched an internal groan that echoed inside of me. What did I get myself into? At one point, he broke down crying, muttering things like how there was no light at the end of the tunnel and that it was all over.

For the next two or so hours, Amy and I tried to talk him through it, convincing him that there were alternatives, that what he had in his mind was not the only "way." Amy then had to contact his emergency contact, which was his dad (he still lived at home). We put his dad on speaker phone to talk to his son, and through his broken English and thick Chinese accent, the dad tried to tell his son that everything would be okay and that he just needed to come home.

The young man didn't say anything. He didn't reply. There was silence; long bouts, awkward bouts, and nervous bouts with a lot of nothing. The dad, at one point, told us that it would be okay and that his son just needed time.

The call ended, and we weren't sure what to do. The young man said that he couldn't even bear to look his father in the eye after losing his job.

After the agony of waiting for an end unclear, I then came up with the idea that I, along with Amy, would help him update his resume and figure out how to find him a new job. Of course, this was something that our company doesn't do, and in fact, it wasn't what any company that I knew of would have done. But that day, we needed something, which was better than nothing.

Saying that plan to him was enough to snap him out of it, and before long, we were in Amy's office working on his resume with him after I helped him clear out his desk.

Before sending him home, I treated him to lunch at a restaurant nearby while he calmed down. It was the strangest and one of the most anxiety-ridden meals that I have ever had. Early in the lunch, he excused himself to go to the bathroom. What seemed like minutes at first soon felt like hours; at one point, I became so worried about whether he was ever coming back that I was about to get out of my seat and check on him in the bathroom. I remember having images run through my mind of opening the bathroom door only to find his lifeless body on the floor and calling 911 as I frantically prayed under my breath. But that didn't happen.

A few minutes later, he came out, and we had our lunch as I tried to make awkward conversation with him. Feelings of the end of the world, of emotional serpents and wolves, shadowed my mind.

The day ended with me driving his car home with him seated next to me as Amy followed us in her car. We couldn't trust him to drive home by himself, not after what had happened.

I tried my best to tell him how much we cared about him and how I wanted things to be okay. I struggled because it's not like there was a company handbook for things like this, and honestly, I was just trying to give him more than the fact that today, he lost his job.

I guess, being where I was, I just started asking him whether he believed in God. He didn't. So I asked him if he would consider the possibility that God might exist, and he replied back that he would.

I then told him about what I believed was real. God came down as Jesus because humanity sinned, and in trying to redeem the world, He died for their sins. If you accepted and believed this, you would be saved, and there would be a better afterlife for you when it was all over. I asked if he was willing to consider whether any of that was real. He said yes, and with that, I said the sinner's prayer with him as I drove him home in his own car. The sinner's prayer is a Christian prayer someone says as an outward method of accepting the salvation God gives.

I know people argue over God and religion. I know that believing in something when there is so much that doesn't make sense is difficult. But the one thing I did grasp at that moment was that this guy needed something. Because his other alternative was nothing — complete, absolute, unforgiving, uncompromising oblivion. And oblivion is a scary thing.

We eventually got him home, and almost at the exact moment Amy and I came into his house, his father was there, greeting us with sliced watermelon. Hanging on the walls nearby, besides a few Chinese calligraphy paintings, were decorated pictures of Mao Zedong.

The father immediately tried to show us an old video of the young man as a child, performing in what seemed to be a recital, as we tried to politely explain to him that his son just wasn't "right" for the job in the nicest way possible. The father was trying so hard, and I think to some level, everyone in the room realized that. By then, the young man had already gone to his room, and we were with the father, trying to politely excuse ourselves. He even gave us gifts of lotion, tea, and shampoo in Victoria's Secret bags. The situation was so surreal that we couldn't help but accept his gifts and then make our way out.

On the way back to the office, while I was riding in Amy's car, she explained to me that she was thinking of calling 911 when he talked about suicide in my office. But then she decided against it because if that happened, he would have most likely been physically restrained, led out of the office, and placed on suicide watch, which would have made a scene. It could have made things worse.

When we both got back, my supervisor, Heather, found out about what had happened. It was already late afternoon, and she told me that I could take the rest of the day off.

My head was spinning by the time I got back to my apartment. The only thing I could do was sit on my couch and stare at the blank TV screen for hours, even after the sun set and everything was dark. I don't even remember turning on any lights until much later that night. I just found it so hard at the time to believe that what I had just gone through was real. It was a strange and disembodied feeling because, on one level, I knew that I should have seen what just happened as a "win," but so much of it felt like a loss.

Oblivion is a scary thing.

* * *

According to the tour guide, the Hallgrímskirkja church was designed to resemble a geyser. Though it's not the oldest church in Iceland, it's one of the most prominent ones. Apparently, in Iceland, the separation of church and state never happened, so the moment you're born, you're automatically registered as a member of the Church of Iceland. Of course, later on, you can choose to unregister and join another religion or abstain, but this appears to be the tradition.

No separation of church and state. I never thought of what that would be like until now: to have them be one and the same thing.

While I was sitting there contemplating, my hand instinctively touched my neck, and I could feel the cloth string around it leading to the metallic cross at the end. I grasped the cross in my palm, harder than usual, until I felt its shape imprint itself in my hand, stinging the inside of it, almost on the verge of forming its own type of stigmata.

I remember that the Book of John, from the Bible, mentions how believers are in the world but not of the world. It's like saying that there can be a separation between the world and what you believe internally, but being in the world is also inevitable. There can be a separation, but also there cannot be a separation.

Like an island of ice and fire, with glacial ice on top and volcanic fire beneath, they still coexist as one.

* * *

By the time I came back to the hotel later that evening, it was getting dark, and after a quick shower, I went down to the hotel restaurant by the lobby to join some of the other members of my tour group. It was the final night before the flight home.

Over the past week, we had grown close to one another with all of the sightseeing and short conversations.

Unlike the city tour group earlier that day, most of this tour group who were with me on the road around the island were from the States. At the table where I had dinner on was a couple from New Jersey. I think their names were Douly and Marianne. They owned a screen door business and were in the process of passing the business down to their sons. Another older couple there was from Virginia, around the DC area; they recommended the soup to me.

As we sat, we talked about the UNESCO heritage site we visited the other day and how even though parts of it were scenic, it honestly didn't impress me compared with all the other sites we'd been to. Supposedly, the biggest thing about this site is that it's the oldest parliamentary site in the world; Iceland's parliament had since been moved to Reykjavik.

Interestingly enough, the man who recommended the soup to me thought of it differently. He said that to him, it was not so much a disappointment of scenery, but rather it was the country's way of telling visitors that this place was very significant to them, even though it might

13

not impress outsiders. I could respect that. I found out later in the conversation that the man who told me this was also a retired Anglican pastor; I think that came out because he noticed that I silently prayed before having the soup he recommended. Funny how things happen.

As we all sat there and talked, we talked about family, the moments we enjoyed on the trip, and the wonderful food that we ate. Douly and Marianne made a commitment to try out the Icelandic hot dog that was all the buzz before heading off to their flight the next day. I had recommended it to them.

Douly, the more cynical of the two, at one point mentioned some of the hang-ups he had concerning his sons, but I could tell there was still a lot of love there, albeit patiently tested love.

At the end of the night, as I was headed back to my room, I recalled one night when some people from my tour group and I went out after dinner to look for the Northern Lights. We tried about two or three separate nights, with little to no success. The best view we got was what looked like a cloud that maybe appeared green in photos, but that was about it.

I remember that as I was walking through a field, when I looked up, I saw the Milky Way for the first time. But amazingly, as beautiful as it was, I took it in stride, probably because I was so focused on wanting to see the Northern Lights. I was so distracted with an expectation that I missed the reality of what I was actually seeing.

On my first trip to Iceland, three years before, I was in a boat sailing outside of the city, and though it would have been unlikely that I would have seen the Northern

Lights, they appeared at one point, exploding over the sky in brilliance.

They were like waves of undulating yellow green; you looked at them as though looking up from the sea floor to the sunlight dancing on the ocean surface. And as I looked, I could feel the burning sting of cold sleet on my face, but the beauty was so immense and grand that it didn't matter. The beauty of it surpassed the pain. It was like the sky was speaking to us in a visual tongue, the tongue of angels, as it covered the entire curve of the atmosphere. This lasted for several minutes, but those minutes felt like hours.

It was a miracle. And the one thing that was in the back of my mind almost the entire time was how much I didn't deserve this.

As I fumbled, sitting on my bed, to place a few items into my carry-on for the flight home tomorrow, I found myself with my travel journal in hand, my thumb already against a worn opening in it. Almost instinctually, I opened it up, and the page that revealed itself was that exact night in March 2016. There I wrote:

"When I went back inside the ship's cabin area, my mind poured over all the things that had to have happened for this moment to come about. You see, earlier the other night, I received a text from an acquaintance, saying that in these past few days, there was increased solar activity from the sun, making this the best time to see the Northern Lights.

But many other things had to have happened too:

1.) The window to see the Lights only occurs September through March in Iceland. I had to have the right date and time to schedule it. Anything outside of this window would have made it impossible.

2.) The weather had to come together at the right time and place; otherwise, either the trip was cancelled or, if not, the clouds would have prevented any sight of the Lights at all. It was also forecast that night to be cloudy with rain or snow!

3.) I was late to the boat, according to the scheduled time that I was supposed to be there, and I could have easily missed it. Had the bus driver to the marina decided to take another route or decided to drop off people in a different order, or if the boat had left on time, I would have missed it altogether!

4.) The increased solar activity just happened to occur on the same day(s) that I scheduled the Northern Lights tour!

5.) When the trip was first cancelled, I was almost resigned to the idea of not rescheduling, given that I had less than two days left in Iceland. But then I suddenly had the idea to reschedule it for the next night.

6.) The boat tour was available for booking for the next day, even though other factors could have easily made it unavailable (such as overbooking or lack of schedule openings)."

Looking at the bottom margin of that journal entry, I saw scribbled, "I see You," and right below that was a reply: "I see you."

Seeing the Northern Lights was one of the most life-changing experiences I ever had. I remember it now, and having it happen once when it could have not happened at all was enough.

I remember reading that one of the reasons why it would be difficult or even near impossible to see the Lights in the city or in the daylight was because of the excess light. In order to see them, it would have to be a dark night, and you would have to be away from any light pollution. Ideally, you would need a backdrop of true black.

I heard that the color of true black is hard to achieve in physical form. Supposedly, it took a team of NASA engineers to develop a material that reproduced that color through nanotechnology. That material would help them see things previously unseen, which I would imagine, those things being made noticeable by their contrast against its darkness. The darkness was necessary to see what needed to be seen.

Although this time in Iceland, I didn't see the Lights as I did the first time, I began remembering all the other things that happened, the little "Milky Way" moments throughout the journey.

I remember seeing the Skogafoss waterfall for the first time and trying to get a close-up shot of it, only to get sprayed by its tumbling waters in the silliest and most wonderful way.

I remember that same day that I went up the staircase to reach the top of those falls, only to have a seventy-something-year-old Douly beat me to the top (I need to lose weight).

And I also remember how I had a great conversation with Mattie, who was in Iceland for the first time, and how afterwards she just fell in love with its beauty, even though she was more used to holidays at tropical destinations. I remember being so happy for her.

In my hotel room at the end of my journey, I had come to a sudden revelation about why I came back. I needed to be reminded of something that was elusive and so easily forgotten as a Milky Way sighting on the way to some greater expectation on a grassy field in the middle of nowhere.

And it wasn't enough to just read what had happened in the past. I needed to be here again. I needed to walk the streets here again. I needed to physically be here for myself and realize that I am alive and being alive to do all of this was a gift on its own.

When it comes to Ragnarök, I've read that there's actually a variation to that Norse myth. Some say it's the true ending of the story. After the war, after all is destroyed, including a majority of the gods, a new world, beautiful and fertile, rises out of the depths. Certain gods, including Thor's sons, will survive and live happily in the new world. Also in this new world are a man and a woman. The man's name is Lif and the woman's name is Lifthrasir. Translated, they respectively mean "life" and "striving after life." The two of them will then populate the earth, reborn and new.

I believe in life, and I believe in the resurrection. I also believe in redemption. And I believe that life is ultimately about believing in something, and belief cannot be separated from life, no matter how much you try. If and when you lose sight of that, can there ever be a light at the end of the tunnel?

As I stuffed the last piece of dirty laundry into my suitcase, I sat back and looked out the window. Nearby, I saw a massive, docked ship drawn up from the water's edge to have its bottom surface repainted and restored. Earlier that week, that same ship's bottom seemed rusted with old and chipping paint. But now, the deep dark red of the lower half showed a fresh coat of paint and looked good as new. Of course, they didn't have to do that. What would be the point of it if that ship's bottom would inevitably get rusted again? But if they didn't do it, the lower part of the hull would degrade. Cracks or fissures might start appearing. And before long, the ship would sink. Though a ship is, in the end, just a ship, the lives on board matter, and if all that could've been done to save them was to do a monthly hull-up, a repainting and resurfacing, then that long, hard process was small by comparison with the need.

Good things have their place and so do bad things. And, just like this trip, just because good things end doesn't mean they're pointless. Just because bad things happen doesn't mean that good things can never happen and that it's the end. Life is suffering but isn't fully defined by it. I choose to believe this. And as long as there is life, there is still choice, and where there is choice, there is still hope.

Pausing for a moment, before finishing the last of my packing, I opened up my travel journal again. Scrawled throughout its pages were various memories, including short mentions, here and there, from my current trip: the first taste of salted licorice ice cream from an ice cream place in Reykjavik, the sky-blue water of the Blue Lagoon, and so on. When I reached the end of my final entry, I took out my pen, and in the margin I wrote, "I see You," followed by the response, "I see you."

2021

Written 1/2/21

It's the day after New Year's Day at the time I'm writing this. The general sentiment in the air is good riddance to 2020, with a limited optimism haunted by foreboding uncertainty.

The ball drop in Times Square was done with only about 40 select guests present, while everyone else watched it be televised. My friends and I celebrated the New Year over Zoom, trying our best to have some degree of joy even in the midst of the awkwardness of it all. This is the first time something like this has happened on such a grand scale. The number of daily deaths in the US from COVID in December surpassed 3,600 lives, which is more than the people lost in 9/11.

One vaccine from Pfizer had come out, and another from Moderna, and distribution of these vaccines had begun last month. My brother, who's a doctor, got his vaccination about two weeks ago. But so far, only about 3 million people have been vaccinated in the US, which is far below the 20 million that the government initially aimed for by the end of the year. A new, more infectious strain of COVID has appeared in the US, with the UK being the first to report it, and there's a degree of uncertainty about whether the vaccines can handle this strain.

It's hard to nail down how I feel about this, knowing that despite the fact that the vaccine is now out, that the pandemic is still far from over. I've heard that most people will not get the vaccine until as late as June 2021. I've spent my holiday vacation these past two weeks in

21

my apartment, mostly in my room streaming movies, watching TV shows, playing games, and writing every now and then to whittle down each day as though it was a type of passive-aggressive labor. These past few months, every once in a while, I've just gone out to my car and sat there, just to be away from everything and be outside. During those moments, I haven't had a premeditated time limit for how long I sit there (at least as far as I know). One day, I think I sat in my car until sunset. Partially, this was because I wanted personal space away from my roommate (no offense to him), but I think at some level, I missed just having somewhere to go. It's hard to tell.

But if there was one thing that I could grab onto in the dark isolation of quarantine it was this: thankfulness. I still had a job. I still had my health. I still had a place to live. And most of all, I still had the ones I love. It's too easy to become bitter and cynical. Some days, it could be like fighting gravity itself: like climbing a steep, flat-faced mountain, with your muscles tense and burning as you desperately cling to whatever openings and cracks your feet and hands can lock into. In these times, the easiest thing to do would be to let go, to let yourself succumb to the fatigue, the ache, and the fire in your body, but at the cost of falling to a certain death. Of course, this is not physical death, but something more nefarious in its own right; a subtle character erosion, when personal virtue and goodness diminish into nothing.

It is the duty of every person to recognize that we affect each other even when we're alone; we are interconnected even when not blood-related because the character we mold in adversity will affect others in the long run when the long run comes. This is not to say that we should pretend, when we communicate with each other during dark times, by putting on a perpetual happy face as we sacrifice honesty on the altar of denial. But it is just to say that we have the right to allow ourselves to feel these things and express them, but then we should choose hope and mercy for ourselves regardless of the darkness. In fact, I am writing this now simply to be honest and to be hopeful by choice, as this is the mercy that I can give myself. This is my confession without the priest or the confession booth. This is the least I can do for myself on this level, in this way, on this day.

Weekly, I try to make it an obligation to write something because the alternative of forgetting and giving up outweighs being dutiful to oneself in whatever way one can. These next few months will be long; I already anticipate the fallout of infections from the holiday week to come in the next few days. I look up at the mountain above me, and I do not see the peak. But at this moment, I will wedge myself into any small opening I can find and let my muscles rest, even when locked into a narrow space. I will not let go. I refuse to fall. And I choose to secure myself in the harness of thankfulness locked by the clamps of faith and the willingness to know that there has been good, that there still is good, and that there will be good things to come.

Deduction 1

If it's helpful, does it make it moral?

If it feels good, does it mean it's good for you?

If you don't care, does it mean it's not important?

If one speaks louder than another, does it mean that his voice should be more heard?

If it's not broken, does it always mean you shouldn't fix it to make it better?

If you're stuck, does it always mean that it's the end of the world?

If it's the end of the world, does it mean that it's the end of right and wrong?

If you struggle, does that always mean you're weak?

If you're weak, does it always mean you can never be strong?

If someone's mean to you, does it mean that they're always bad?

If someone's nice to you, does it mean that they're always good?

If something doesn't make you happy, does it mean it's bad?

If you have everything you want, does that mean you'll be happier?

If you're happier, does that always mean things will be better?

If happiness is the goal of life, should most people in the world strive for it?

If happiness is the goal of life and most people strive for it, then why isn't the world better?

By Our Own Hand 1/6/2021

The American capitol has been breached.

The capitol had not been breached since 1812, by the British.

This breach was made by Americans.

Americans were the ones who invaded their own capitol.

Some have said that had these people been mostly black, the response would have been different.

Black or white, now five people are dead.

Social media has banned the president.

The president, at one point, wanted to pardon himself before he leaves office.

I can't believe that, in the span of 48 hours or so, the walls of the nation feel like they're burning down in what was once considered the world's greatest country.

What those rioters did was horrible,

Terrible,

And insulting.

But just because I think their actions are horrible, that doesn't make me liberal (I'm not).

Though I'm conservative, that doesn't make me a Republican (I'm actually unaffiliated).

These things shouldn't matter, but people will somehow make them matter. As far as who these "people" are: take your pick.

I'm angry. I'm upset. And I'm ashamed.

I'm American.

E pluribus unum.

"Out of many, one."

We are many

But how much longer must we not be one?

A Perspective on Suffering

Written 2/6/21

It's the end of the first week of February 2021, and much has happened since the beginning of the year. On January 6, the US capitol was violently breached for the first time since 1812, when it was breached by the British. A total of five people ended up dead. New mutated strains of COVID variants have now been found in the US and, from what I can tell, there are at least two of them, one from the UK and another from South Africa. The current death toll in the US is around 450,000.

There's news that a second stimulus check is coming to people, but it's still going through Congress. We'll see what happens. Just the previous month, after registering for the COVID vaccination, I got a notification a little while ago that I've been grouped into Group 1c for vaccination and, right now, it's a matter of getting an appointment notification, which still hasn't happened. The latest news is that there hasn't been enough vaccine distribution to get everyone vaccinated quickly, and it appears that frustration is boiling over.

This past week or so, I've been thinking a little bit about the Buddhist idea that "life is suffering". Actually, this concept is based more on the first of the four noble truths of Buddhism and is often one of the more misunderstood ones. Reader, please bear in mind that I don't claim to be an expert on Buddhism, let alone a master of any of its intricacies. But something I do understand from the little that I know is that one of its main goals is to reach an enlightened state where all suffering ends through various practices.

This idea does strike me as something inspiring, but at the same time, as contrary to my own Christian faith. Overall, though, I must agree with the notion that life is suffering.

Suffering is unavoidable in this world. And yes, suffering can be lessened with the right choices. Suffering can also be alleviated with compassion and community. But it is impossible for anyone, regardless of what walk of life they come from, to avoid it completely all of the time. To ever hold the idea that there is such a perpetual existence where suffering does not exist while we're on this side of heaven is unrealistic. And I think the sooner we come to terms with that, the better off we'll be.

But at the same time, we must also know that all suffering in and of itself is not necessarily bad in the purest sense. From what I know of Buddhism, the goal appears to be to reach an enlightened state where all suffering ceases. But when I observe one of the primary tenets of Christianity (my own faith), where God Himself came down to Earth as a man to totally embrace suffering that wasn't His own, the contrast is striking. In Buddhism it seems that followers progress from an imperfect state to a perfect and higher one. In Christianity, a being who is already at His highest state and who is already perfect comes down to reconcile that which is imperfect, to embrace suffering in its cruelest manner. What shall we make of this?

For the sake of this essay, I'm not here to argue religion per se, but I think one thing that I can argue is that we all need perspective on suffering. Perhaps the goal of life isn't to avoid suffering at all costs but rather to accept it in such a way that a greater good can come from it. There is suffering for good reasons, and there is suffering for bad reasons. We can suffer for the right reasons, whether it's from making sacrifices for others or from carrying on through the pain of an unavoidable crisis for the sake of duty rather than vainly running from it. We can also suffer for the wrong reasons, due to poor choices we've made or paying the penalty for crimes we've committed. The Bible mentions that if we follow Christ, we are required to take up our crosses and follow Him. Again, this is another example of embracing suffering for the right reasons.

But as an aside, I would like to mention that not all sources of suffering are binary things. Many times, suffering can come from things well beyond our control, regardless of the choices we've made. Sometimes, suffering just is; it is something that just happens without any direct or clear line of blame. In such cases, whether one wishes to define suffering as something for the good or for the bad will rely heavily, if not entirely, on how we choose to respond to that suffering. And that brings me to the next point.

Much bad has happened in 2021, and it's barely even two months in. I have come to accept the fact that we live in a fallen, broken world filled with fallen and broken people, including myself. I have come to accept the fact that, yes, life is suffering, and I shouldn't expect anything less. But I've also come to accept that I need perspective in perceiving all that has happened. There are many more people who have it far worse than me in this world. I have the privilege of being born into an upper-middle-class family in one of the most well-to-do nations in the world, even though at this point, things seem to be going downhill for the nation. I do not have to fight each day just to be able to have food that day. I do not have to worry that if I get cut or injured, an infection could kill me. I have access to some of the best medicine in the world. I am privileged, and to say otherwise, that somehow my life is filled with cruelty, would be an insult to everyone less fortunate than me. But should we leave it at that? I am lucky and nothing more? No, there is more.

With the right acceptance of what's true and the right perspective on what's true, there is still a need for direction. Because I've been given much, because I believe that every man has purpose in light of my spiritual convictions, I must strive to be better each day, even in the smallest ways. Acceptance of what is true and perceiving what is true are incomplete acts without a purpose driving them. For myself, personally, that purpose is to use each day to be productive, not just for myself, but for what is required of me at my job, for what is expected from me by my family, and for what is expected from me by my friends and, most importantly, my God.

Needless to say, I've been far from perfect in all these things. There have been many times where I've been lazy at my job and I have not loved as much as I should when it comes to friendships. There have been times where I have put God on the sidelines and gone about trying to care only about what makes me comfortable. I'm guilty as charged. But thank God for grace. For that reason and other reasons, I'm not giving up, especially considering the way the world is now.

If anything, with the chaos and the madness going on, the urgency to be more responsible and to strive to be better only increases. It's too easy to play victim and, in fact, many times very convenient. But in truth, we are all victims in our own way, and dwelling only on that will mostly bring more harm than good.

Life is suffering. That is true. But for the suffering that is unavoidable or even necessary, I will face it and not deny it. For the suffering that is needless and bad, I will seek to minimize it, not just in my own life but also in the lives of others. I will live deliberately and struggle each day to live in balance, not only with my own needs but also with the needs of others, even as imperfect as I am. There is nothing or at least very little I can do to change the death toll of COVID or to settle all the political and social unrest in the country, but I can at least control my actions or the way I respond to it all. And the way I plan to respond is with responsibility, truthfulness, and the audacity to live in faith, hope, and love.

Ramming Fists Against the Wall

There was once a man who became so angry and frustrated that he made it a habit each day to ram his fist against a brick wall. On the good days, he did it only once or twice. On really bad days, he would punch it so many times that he lost count. And throughout it all, the only certainty that he had was how much the things going on inside of him overrode the pain shooting up from his knuckles as they made contact with the unyielding cold surface of brick and mortar. Whenever he was asked about the bruises and the scrapes on his knuckles, he would simply say, "I had a rough day." Whenever he was asked if he wanted to talk about it, the best that he would come up with was "No, I'm fine."

It was not enough for the man to feel the pain in his fists. It was not enough for the man to eventually see the marks of knuckle imprints slowly showing up on that wall beneath the layers of stained dried blood. Nothing was ever enough.

By the time the police arrived at his apartment, months later, all they could find was his cold corpse with a note saying, "No, I'm fine."

People have asked, since then, who exactly his punches were meant for. Many would say that he was just angry and didn't know what else to do. That makes sense, but it also doesn't. The man lived alone. He seemed well off and appeared normal by most accounts. But a few people have said his fists were meant for someone in particular. That someone was himself.

I Live

I am alive and, because I am alive, I choose to be grateful.

I am loved regardless of whether the ones who love me are physically here or not.

And even if I don't feel loved, I still choose to love in return.

I have food to eat and water to drink.

And because I can be filled, I choose to give to others,

Even if I don't have money to give.

I have a better self to pursue.

And, because I can be better,

I choose to become better each day and every waking moment

Even when things get worse.

I have a God who gave Himself to me.

And because I have Him, I choose to share Him with others

Even if that means not using words.

I breathe, and because I still breathe,

I choose to strive.

Ode to Professionalism

Dear Mark,

I just want to email you to update you on the latest ProAdtech meeting with ~~these clueless grunts for hire~~ our vendors.

The meeting went well for the most part ~~if you enjoy massive failures~~, but fell short of the company's expectations given ~~how screwed our company is~~ the economic climate of the corporation.

The vendors insisted ~~that we should do all of the work~~ that our team take further initiative and ownership of the 561 project, which, as you know, ~~is a massive dumpster fire~~ already had its challenges earlier this quarter.

We have managed ~~to yell at them until they gave in~~ to negotiate with them to take custody of the medical coding aspect of the project, which is crucial to pharmacovigilance, ~~which I still don't know what these guys do but they sound smart~~ but we need more time to negotiate the contract, which has ~~yet to even be written~~ yet to be finalized.

Over the course of lunch, which we provided for them ~~(we should have told them to brown bag it)~~, we emphasized ~~how useless they were and how little they delivered~~ how important the milestones were for ~~that thing I'm afraid of~~ the interim analyses, and it was hard for them to understand what our team is facing in light of the study's status ~~(because they're idiots)~~.

~~I literally give up.~~ I think we need to escalate this to the senior director at once, given the direction these vendors are going.

~~I desperately need allies, so please back me up.~~ I always appreciate your input as a valued team member.

~~(Generic ending)~~ If you have any further comments, please reach out.

Warmest regards,

David Yuen

~~(impressive title)~~

Senior Data Manager

An Aging Father's Words to His Son

Son, I know we haven't been the best of friends since I've grown older. The other day, when we had that argument in the car because I asked you too many questions about your health, it's only because I care about you. You said you understood that. But when I tried to explain more about why I asked, you only became angrier and angrier. I didn't understand why. I only thought you were angry because you actually didn't understand, and that's why I tried to explain. I don't mean to be this way. But when you get older, you forget things, and you don't remember as well. That's why it didn't surprise me when you said I'd already asked you those questions many times before, even though I thought it was only a few times.

The other day, when you got frustrated at me because you came home early from work to do the laundry and you couldn't find the detergent, I was in the middle of something, and I had no idea that you texted me. I don't always have my phone with me when I'm in the middle of things. And I didn't know that you were doing laundry that day. I'd forgotten to put the detergent back into the closet. I'm sorry. I forget things. And I feel bad that I do. But please know that I don't mean to do it. But even though you know, you still get angry at me anyway. I'll tell you one thing that's hard to forget: how much it hurts to see you feeling this way and knowing that it won't be the last time.

Whenever you say something and I ask you to repeat it, it would really mean a lot if you could just be patient with me. Because when I do ask you to say it again, you not only repeat it, but you scream it, like you were yelling at someone who didn't care enough to hear you the first time. Trust me, I do care, but I can't control my fading ears. I ask you to say it again because I care about what you have to say, not the opposite.

Every time you get angry at me for things that I can't control, it's like telling me to not even bother. It feels like nothing I can say will ever be the right answer for you.

What's obvious to you isn't always obvious to me. I need you to know that even though I don't understand all the expressions you make or the words that you use or the gadgets that you're shocked that I don't get, it makes me feel useless, especially when you sigh and walk away. And when I feel useless like that, I sometimes wish I could crawl away and become invisible.

I don't mean to make you angry. I don't mean to make you frustrated. But please, it's hard for me. All I ask is for just a little respect and dignity. I only get angry back at you because I don't know what else to do.

Age takes away far more than it gives. And having a good relationship with my own son is the least that I can ask for, even when I don't know how and I'm also scared of asking. Someday you'll understand, but I'd rather you understand now and not later.

You're still my son. I still love you, even though I'm not good at showing it. You still have your mother's eyes. But unfortunately, you have my habit of frustration. I want things to be better between us. I'll try harder. But I wish you could show me that you'll try harder too.

A Son's Words to His Aging Father

Dad, I'm trying my best. The times I get angry at you, you know I don't mean it. But sometimes it's not easy for me.

I know that you care about me, but you don't have to keep reminding me that I need to remember this or that or that I should check this or that because I know these things already. Telling me these things and asking me these things again and again doesn't help.

And even when I try to tell you things and answer your questions and you don't hear me, again and again, I just don't know what to do. Honestly, I can't tell whether you really don't hear me or if you're actually not trying hard enough to listen.

When you come to me, again and again, to ask me how to do something that I've already shown you how to do, do you realize how frustrating that is? And the next day, you just do it again. Were you even paying attention to me the first three times? Do you care enough to even remember or listen to what I've said?

You seem to have a problem with listening to me. Yes, I know about your hearing. But show me that you're actually trying. I can't read your mind.

Dad, I miss the days when things were simpler. I hate the fact that once I get back from work, I'm too tired to answer you or to show you that I care. I hate and regret the way I treat you sometimes. Don't get me wrong. I should've been more patient when you asked me about how to send an email. I shouldn't have raised my voice when you asked me about what I've been eating lately or the fact that you broke your recliner for the third time this month and need me to fix it.

It's just so hard trying to get through a workday and then helping you with the same things. Back then, I wish you would have just told me how hard things were when I was young and why you sometimes didn't have time for me. Actually, I think you did. But you did it in your own way. It's always been in your own way.

I just want things to be smooth between us. I know I can seem as if I'm upset with you. But I just get so tired sometimes, and the last thing I need is you hounding me about something or with a question I don't have the answer for, but you assume that I do just because I'm young.

I love you, Dad. Really, I do. I'm trying my best. But sometimes, I wish I knew for sure that you were doing the same.

The Lessons So Far

Written 3/17/21

It's Saint Patrick's Day 2021. All three COVID vaccines are being administered: one from Moderna, another from Pfizer, and the latest from Johnson and Johnson, which, unlike the other two vaccines, only requires one injection rather than two separate ones.

The clock was sprung forward for daylight savings three days back, and the extra daylight seemed appropriate with more of the vaccines being distributed in the US. But there's still a long way to go before most of the population has been vaccinated.

My mom and dad had their first of two injections this month; my mom got the Moderna vaccine, and my dad got the Pfizer one. The good thing is that they experienced few side effects besides a sore arm that lasted a day or two. Today, I was working with a friend of mine to secure a possible appointment for myself to get vaccinated, and we got two close calls where an appointment was in reach, but we missed them. We'll keep trying in the coming days.

It's a very odd time right now because it's a time of transition. Things seem hopeful, and I've gotten word that things may be close to normal as soon as April, but I doubt it, even though I hear that more people in my circle of friends are getting vaccinated. It was the one-year anniversary last Thursday, on March 11, when COVID was declared a global pandemic by the World Health Organization. With this, the more I think about what's happening and what has happened, the more I consider the things I've been learning this past year since everything started. Right now, we're far from the finish line. But it's worth thinking back and seeing what lessons have made themselves apparent. I can think of some offhand.

1. Be thankful for what you have because things can easily be worse.

I believe I once saw a news report where a doctor said that if you're still alive at the beginning of this new year, then last year wasn't that bad. It's bad enough that things have gotten bad for many others, with the death of loved ones or the loss of job security or any means of income. But things could have easily gotten worse for so many more people. I'm so fortunate to have what I have and not to have suffered as greatly as many others have in this world.

2. If you have been blessed and fortunate enough not to have suffered as much as others, do what you can to pay it forward.

In light of how much I've been given and how much I realize how fortunate I am compared with others, I need to be more proactive in giving more, helping more, and appreciating more. And not just that, perhaps more importantly, I need to learn to complain less. Complaining when you are so fortunate not only displays entitlement but also a lack of gratitude that steals the joy from your life and from the lives of others around you.

3. Realize how much you've taken things for granted and how true the saying really is that the grass is greener on the other side.

Before the pandemic, when I had to trudge into the office every weekday with little exception, the idea of working from home would most likely have been so idealized in my mind that to have that happen each day would have been heaven on earth. Now, after months of working from home, day in and day out, I actually begin to cherish the days when I had to go into the office to get onsite things done. But it's funny that when this pandemic is over, and things come closer to normal again, I most likely will begin to wish that I were working from home again. If I'm going to retain anything, it should be more appreciation for even the littlest things (even if it's the frustration of the daily commute!).

4. Community is something worth investing in, even when it's inconvenient.

During this pandemic, I had to go through a move to a new place, the struggle and stagnation of isolation, the juggle of keeping tabs on my aging parents while working remotely, and random things that would come up every now and then. I found that, even in the midst of a pandemic, my community stepped in to help me at almost every step. And in turn, I have been blessed to contribute to others in my community in return. Yes, helping others can be inconvenient because sacrifice, by definition, should be inconvenient (or else it wouldn't be sacrifice). But I have found that, had I not had this community, which I in turn have invested in, things would have been much harder and perhaps worse.

5. Hardship reveals our weaknesses. And that's not a bad thing.

This year, I've learned a lot of inconvenient truths about myself. I'm prone to anxiety more than I thought. I tend to panic and mess up because that's what I do. I tend not to be on top of things that I should be on top of, and this happens too often. And I doubt myself too much. But had there not been this pandemic, then I would either not have taken these weaknesses seriously enough or I might not have discovered them this year. Imagine if I discovered these much later in life, when things about myself were harder to change or when time was no longer on my side.

6. Love others and appreciate them more because you never know when the next thing might happen.

Around this time, I would usually cook a corn beef dinner for my Christian fellowship and probably tell them about how that tradition started for the hundredth time. During those times, cooking that several-hours-long dinner for so many people was very stressful, but in the end, nearly every time, it ended in success and happiness for those I love. This year, the only corn beef dinner I've made so far was one I delivered to my pastor and his family. I'm hoping to make another dinner for myself and my roommate, but it's a far cry from what it used to be. Love the people who are in your life and who share it with you because anything could happen. For your sake and others', try to see things in the long term and not the short term.

Just Maybe

I always wondered why God created certain places to have unique seasons, whereas other places wouldn't. I wondered if God would have allowed seasons in the Garden of Eden, when things were sinless and death had no reign.

I think it's to make us appreciate more of what we have and to force us to think more before we act, so that we can become better versions of ourselves (if we allow it). In nearly every part of the world, there's still a season of harvest, regardless of how hot or cold it gets, with some exceptions.

People still need to prepare. People still need to find beauty in things when they're there and then also when they're gone.

Yet even in the most extreme conditions, there are people who live there. Tribes are settled in the Sahara. Tribes dwell in the arctic. Despite these unspeakable challenges, humanity still thrives against all odds. Cultures still develop, and customs come into being, even under the worst conditions.

God created us in His image. And if His image is an indication of anything, despite our sin and despite how bad things get, then one thing's for sure: God can still work in the worst cases, with the worst of things.

If the evidence of His image and, therefore, His goodness through people can thrive even in the horrors of war, the horrors of the environment, and the horrors of limited resources, can it be fair to say that God Himself can, therefore, do more?

We need each other. As much as we hate. As much as we accuse. As much as we blame. We need one another. But it's too easy to overlook, too easy to dismiss, and too easy to take for granted the issue of relationships, when relationships are so hard and sometimes too simple.

Must we always be at each other's throats, either literally or in our minds, the moment insecurity strikes? We humans are amazing and frightening things at once. Our ingenuity, our ambition, our brilliance, and our stupidity make us formidable, pitiful, and awe-inspiring at once. There is drama to be had in all this.

The universe is vast. Our lives, in the light of the grand scheme, are flickers of nothing that only last a moment before vanishing into the hereafter. It is easy to think that we're a huge accident.

But I challenge those who read this to consider that perhaps the braver thing is not to overstate our insignificance, but to deny it fully: to propel ourselves toward the fact that we are the opposite. That maybe, just maybe, each of us are heroes destined for great and noble things, if only we'd allow it.

Death to Self

I will bring myself to heel and force my flesh to submit to my will.

I will beat the selfishness out of my own heart.

With equal effort and sound mind, I will force myself to move beyond myself.

I will break down the barriers known as comfort and apathy.

To myself, I bring forth my will and bind my fears.

My fears are an illusion, and I will force myself through them.

Their whispers hold no power. Their influence has no sway.

They will not keep me from loving others.

They will not bind me to themselves.

I am not a slave to them and, scream as they might,

I will be fearless in my love and fearless with my love. I will be laborious in my duty to live for others.

Sloth, away from me! Indulgence, know your place!

I will die to myself.

Though perfect I will not be, it's enough to know that it has already been done by the One who came before me.

Deduction 2

If things are going to get dirty again, what's the point of always cleaning them?

If things are eventually going to break and wear out, what's the point of maintaining them?

Why do you continue to eat and drink if you will only get hungry and thirsty again?

When you eat and drink, even though you do it over and over again, do you still find happiness when you do these things?

When you finish cleaning, do you still, at times, find satisfaction when things are clean?

Why do we complain about the big and grandiose things if we cannot handle even the small and menial things?

Just because something is small or menial, does that necessarily mean that it's unimportant?

Just because a person has a job that is "small" and menial, does it mean that he or she is unimportant?

There are many people who have jobs considered "small" and menial, but why are a lot of them called "essential"?

Why do we quickly judge things, even when we know little about the things we judge?

Why do we quickly judge people, even when we often know little about the people we judge?

Regardless of the Rain

Written 3/25/21

It was Wednesday, March 24, 2021, when I took an Uber to the Meadowlands Arena around 5 p.m. I don't remember ever going inside that arena before other than passing by it a few times from the outside. I think this was my first time to actually see it on the inside.

It took a little effort to direct the driver, once he got inside the maze of roads and vacant parking lots nearby. I needed to get to "Lot M," according to the vaccination appointment email that I had received. On the way, we passed by the recently opened "American Dream" complex that was supposed to be some kind of supermall/tourist destination spot that took years to complete. There were some cars there, but almost everywhere else around us, the area looked empty from left to right.

Eventually, I pointed out the lit-up construction signs scrolling the words "vaccinations" and "Lot M" to the driver. He didn't see it at first. Fortunately, there were one or two cars ahead of us that appeared to be going toward the spot where the signs were directing them, so I told him to follow them. Eventually, by the time we came to the second blinking sign, the driver saw it, and Lot M was in sight—the one lot in the Meadowlands arena filled with cars.

The sky was gray and overcast. After being dropped off, I walked toward the entrance of the arena, and almost immediately, I saw the National Guardsmen dressed in their camo fatigues, directing people on the line to the entrance.

Supposedly, they had opened up the Meadowlands Arena to act as one of many vast vaccination sites around the country that would help get the maximum number of people vaccinated against COVID as quickly as possible. I remembered from the news a few days back that slightly less than a third of the American population had received at least their first dose. This was going to be my first one, and I wasn't exactly sure what to expect. From a friend of mine who already received both his doses (he was NYPD, and I think he got the Moderna one), he said that the first shot wasn't much, but the second shot, which you get a few weeks later, felt like getting hit by a truck. Mind you, I wasn't worried. I was more concerned about wanting to get this thing over with and wondering when things would go back to normal again.

Since my appointment was at 5:10 p.m., one of the people in line mentioned to me that they already called that group in, so I could skip ahead. I appreciated it. I went ahead to the guardsmen at the doorway, who ushered me to a long hallway ramp into the building proper.

When I entered the building, I could already see banners and posters saying things like "Welcome Change Starts Here" and so on and so forth. The first glimpse of the interior of the arena reminded me of something like a cafeteria or an airport lounge, which was welcoming enough. I think that in pre-pandemic times, this would have been where the tickets and refreshments were sold, but obviously, tickets and refreshments were not for sale today.

When I was there, a myriad of thoughts randomly ran through my mind. This was historic. I should start taking pictures. Oops, wait, there's a big sign that says we can't take pictures. One of the guardsmen, who caught me doing so, just told me to delete my pictures. Sorry, my bad. The funny thing was that as soon as I began doing it, a girl next to me started to do it too. When the guardsmen warned me, the girl told me she got the idea from me, and I laughed it off, saying I just wanted to do it because it felt historic. She smiled back, knowing where I was coming from.

Either way, this wasn't anything small. The gravity of where I was and what I was getting was clear. As I grabbed a serial card, I was led to the first processing booth in a room filled with other booths that had people behind makeshift desks and computers. Thoughts kept coming into my mind, not in any particular order.

What would it be like telling generations afterwards about taking the first COVID vaccine? Especially, many years later, when taking the COVID vaccine becomes no different than taking the flu shot every flu season? Would they wonder about how big of a deal it was for us, or just shrug their shoulders and go back to their same old, same old? I'm guessing probably the latter, but I guess that would depend on the person.

After processing, I lined up for the actual vaccination, which took me through a zigzag line roped off by ribbon dividers. It reminded me of waiting in line after coming out of an airport gate to get processed for entry back into the country. I missed traveling. I missed flying to another place, even if it was just another part of the US. I wondered how long it would be before things can return back to the way they were. I guessed not for a while, even after most people got vaccinated. Yes, travel might come back, but the world I knew was long gone, and the constant reminder of potential infection would stay with us.

I felt sad about it. I felt hopeful that soon things would ease up. I felt focused, in a weird way, in my determination to do my part and be responsible for my part, whatever that might be. I looked at the other people in line. There were people who were old, people who were young, people who were overweight, and people who were skinny. People of different ethnicities, all in civilian clothes, juxtaposed with the camouflaged guardsman and uniformed health care workers, making efforts to run things smoothly. When my turn came up, I was directed to station 5 (I think it was station 5), where the health-care worker asked me to prepare my arm. I then asked her which arm to prepare and she said that I got to choose. I undid my shirt, and I chose my right arm.

She then told me that I was getting the Pfizer vaccine as she was preparing the syringe. And just like that, after a sharp pinch, I got the shot. I thanked her and got my paperwork together and went to the observation section of the arena, where they said I needed to stay there for a self-timed 15 minutes before I could leave.

The observation area wasn't much besides a sectioned-off area with spaced apart folding chairs facing a TV that had a health-care worker talking about the vaccine, I assumed (the volume was really low, so I couldn't hear anything). Sitting in that chair, I started the timer on my phone, as the soreness of my arm reminded me of what just happened. That soreness will stay with me for a bit. I then sent my pastor a quick email telling him I just got the shot, along with the scheduled date my second dose and the symptoms I felt, just so he could keep a tally of everyone in my fellowship.

The paperwork they handed me had a cute sticker on it saying, "I MADE COVID-19 HISTORY." Huh . . . that's cute . . . and hopeful. We all need that hope. I'm glad I did what I did. I know there's an anti-vaxxer movement out there, and the idea of it sounded ridiculous to me on this side of the tunnel. I understood their point about feeling forced into doing something they didn't want to do, for whatever reason. But honestly, the more I thought about it, the more I really didn't want to go into that. I just wanted to focus on this, where I was, when I was.

It was raining heavily by the time I left the arena, and my Uber driver arrived to pick me up. My roommate was notified only a day or two ago that one of his coworkers in his office, which he had been going to on a regular basis, had a family member that tested positive for COVID. Since then, my roommate had been in isolation and, today, the day I was getting vaccinated, was the day he was going to get tested to see if he was positive or not, using the one car we had between us. The timing was almost impeccable. I hoped things would turn out all right for him.

The rain was relentless on the drive home. It made everything damp and miserable, especially by the time I got back and had to walk to my front door. At that point, I was hungry, wet, and tired. My arm was sore, and the rain seemed like it was going to last all night.

But then again, it was only rain. Nothing permanent. Nothing disastrous. It was just another phase in existence. And in due time, the sky would clear, and the sun would be back out again for a new day. I would have dinner soon and realize that my life was better than I thought, even though it didn't feel like it at the moment when I was walking through the rain. Our lives are filled with a myriad of isolated moments, all lined up together, both good and bad. But they come and go. And history, even the most major points, is made of those moments chosen (by us, in some cases) and directed by a greater hand. When the door creaked open and I entered the apartment, my roommate was back. We talked for a bit and, later on, I went out to pick up groceries that day, along with some dinner for my roommate. Life continued, regardless of the rain.

The Lazy Workaholic

There was once a man who spent his life moving from one task to another, checking off items from a list that he had in his mind. After each item was checked off, usually a new item would appear. But the funny thing was, even when everything on his list was checked off and there was nothing left to do, he would despair in his boredom and his restlessness. And even when he had items on his lists, he wouldn't be happy either because he had no peace as long as there were tasks to be done that weren't done yet. There was no in-between, no compromise to be given, just the anxiousness of not getting enough done or the frustrated boredom when everything was done, which then led back to anxiety. Eventually, everything became an item on his list, even fun things, like hanging out with friends, watching a movie by himself, or going on vacations.

Eventually, this man got married. That was one box he could check off his list. Eventually, this man had a son. That was another box checked off.

But before long, his son had grown older and bitter that his dad was there but not really there for him. And before long, his wife began to feel lonely because she was always treated like she was just some other item to be checked off. It was only then that the man realized his mistake.

You see, it's easy to make lists in your mind. It's easy, even though not all of the time, to get this task done or that task done to make the list shorter. But letting go and realizing that it's all right to not be in control is hard.

It's easy to worry about spreadsheets or projects at work, but it's not so easy to focus on figuring out relationships or the fact that they can always be better and that settling with just "alright" isn't enough. It's easy to worry about things that need to be picked up or bought, but it's not easy to spend time with others to make things right that are wrong. And most of all, it's easy to keep moving so quickly that you never catch up with yourself.

When he was alone, as an older man, the man who had been working all his life finally realized, too late, that his real problem wasn't that he wasn't good at working or at making more work for himself, but rather that he didn't work hard enough on the things that really mattered.

Wooden Castles

There once was a boy who wanted to build a castle of wood that would tower to the sky. It would be the biggest, greatest thing in the world once he was done. So the boy went to work, laboring for days, bringing the planks of wood together, sawing and cutting through what would become its joints. Every day, the boy hammered away, nail after nail, and drilled and worked from morning to sunset. Eventually, a month had passed, and when the boy stepped back to review his work, his heart sunk. The foundation was slanted, the walls were lopsided, and the very planks that he had so tirelessly put together barely held together. The castle he had built for himself was less sturdy than a popsicle stick tower that a breeze could push over.

The boy, in his anger, threw down his hammer and cried in despair as he fell to the ground. "It's not fair! It's not fair!" the boy exclaimed, pounding his fists into the dirt. "How could this have gone wrong?" The boy's thoughts raced as the castle tilted sideways before creaking down to the ground with a slight thump, its joints coming apart one by one. The boy was devastated.

Nearby, the father heard his son. He knew what his son was doing this whole time, and, even before his son began a month earlier, he had asked him whether he wanted his help, but the son insisted on doing it on his own. The father, with a sigh, allowed his son to do what he wanted as he carefully watched from afar to make sure that he would be all right.

But his son wasn't all right, and it was then that the father stepped in, picking his son up off the ground before holding him tightly in his arms.

"I'm here, son," the father said, his tone loving, his arms embracing. "It's all right that the castle was not built. Castle or not, that does not keep you from being my son. I love you, and that hasn't changed. This failure will not stop you from starting again."

With that, the father then carefully helped his son take apart the fallen castle and, with his guiding hand, together they took the remaining pieces and did what they could to build something together.

With his son's hand clasped in his own, the father showed his son how to determine a level plane. With his own tape measure, the father showed his son how to premeasure dimensions even before a nail was set or a cut was made and how to use every tool in the right way. With his kind words, his father directed his son on how to balance functionality with beauty, and by the end of one day, they had built a table and bench together out of what had been rubble.

Gazing at their finished work, together they felt a sense of accomplishment. But the boy was troubled and, without thinking, said what he felt: "But it doesn't feel special. . . . I just wish I had done this on my own."

The father, looking at his son, then said to him, "This is special because you didn't do it on your own. There will be many times in the future when you will do things on your own, whether you like it or not, but there will only be a few times when you get to do things with your father. And someday, when you do need to build castles on your own, you will remember the bench and the table we made. You will remember how to find level planes and how to plan, before even a cut is made, so that your castles will be fine, tall, and sturdy."

It was then that the boy realized the truth of what his father had said. Wooden castles come and go, but principles last a lifetime.

A Second Shot 4/11/21

It was raining on and off throughout that day.

As cars congested the Meadowlands Sports Complex parking lot, things were just a little harder and a little more urgent than usual. There were car horns sounding every now and then, and a cop even showed up at one point.

There were a lot more people here than during the first vaccination. But then again, it was Sunday, a weekend, when everyone would have tried to grab an appointment. There were crowds and lines of people with raincoats and umbrellas, and some people like me, with neither.

They were running late today, and even though it was already getting toward 11 a.m., they were still calling people who had been scheduled for 10:30 a.m. or earlier to line up. Everyone else was asked to stay behind the yellow barriers until they were called. Reservists in full fatigues were yelling at times to reiterate where the groups were supposed to stand and even rebuked the crowd for failing to line up single file.

I'm sure people were complaining. I'm sure a level of misery was present. But all things considered, all that misery was most likely of the first-world variety.

Was there a little frustration? Yes.

Did it suck that it was raining? Yes.

Was I glad to be here on a Sunday morning? Maybe not.

But was I glad to be here? Yes.

Regardless of who you were and what you thought, what was necessary remained necessary, and life remained the focal point, even when people were still trying to deal with the situation in whatever way they could.

I heard from others that the second dose was a doozy, with all the aches, pains, mild fevers, or worse that may (or may not) follow. It's a small price to pay for a long-term issue that, without a dose, could mean life or death. And yet people still complained.

Today, I wouldn't. Today, I would do what needed to be done.

Count my blessings.

Acknowledge that the rain is needed to make things grow and to contrast with sunny days.

That there is a point for the rain, just as much as there's a point to all of this.

Others less fortunate have it worse. Some don't even get a single shot, let alone a second one, at anything (vaccine or not). And, for their sake, I have no excuse.

On the Derek Chauvin Verdict

Written 4/21/21

Toward the evening of Tuesday, April 20, 2021, the verdict was declared regarding the trial of Derek Chauvin on the death of George Floyd. He was found guilty on all three charges against him, which were manslaughter along with second and third degree murder.

I first found this out after work, and it was practically the first thing that came on my TV the moment I turned it on. It was a breaking news segment at the time, which wasn't a surprise.

As a whole, and from what I understand, I do agree with the verdict, and I do believe justice has been served as result of the evidence and due process, which was needed. Derek Chauvin was tried, the evidence was presented, arguments were made on both sides, and he was found guilty. I'm glad that George Floyd's family received the justice they hoped for, and I hope and pray that there will now be some healing in the nation and with regard to the racial divide.

But in light of all this and in light of the fact that I'm glad this happened, I look upon this with a degree of hesitancy because questions still haunt my mind. When the verdict was read, according to the news agency, many celebrated it as a racial victory. In fact, it was almost as though it was mostly a racial victory. Does this incident involve the issue of race or racial tension? Yes. But to what proportion was race a factor in this? If it was mostly about race, would it thus imply that had George Floyd been white, Derek Chauvin would not have killed him? If this was an African American cop who committed this act on a white man or just on another African American man, would he have been found equally guilty by a jury? And if not, wouldn't that be a big issue, and would it have had as big an impact on the nation? I don't know the answer to these questions.

I would like to think that, had the races been different and the same crime was committed, the same amount of outrage would have been expressed. I would like to think that if such a crime was committed, the same guilty verdicts would have been given regardless of race. But I doubt it would happen that way. And the fact that many people in the public eye do not seem to be addressing this and are quick to label all that happened almost on a purely racial level does trouble me.

But arguably, if this did lead to less racial profiling in law enforcement and, likewise, less community stereotyping of law enforcement (that all cops are bigots), would it be good? Absolutely. If this led to law enforcement reforms such that the police became more effective, efficient, and open to working with the community, would this be a wonderful thing? Yes.

But I believe we should be careful with ourselves before we immediately hop onto the opinion bandwagon without thinking more deeply about it. We should not be quick to assume, and we should be honest about how we feel.

One of the Bible verses that sticks out to me when I think about this was Proverbs 4:27, which tells us to "not turn to the right or the left . . ." and to "keep your foot from evil."

I think I may have mentioned this before in my previous writings, but it's worth mentioning again that I do try my best to keep to this, even when it may not be popular to bring it up at times. When it comes to the George Floyd and Derek Chauvin issue, I think that in our thirst for justice, we could be turning either to the left or the right, but to what degree and in what direction, God only knows.

But it is not irredeemable to stray in our thinking, just as long as we're willing to be corrected. But that can't occur if we're not willing to listen to each other or even to dissenting voices on the matter. And if we choose not to listen and we shut out all dissenting voices completely, without the willingness to have a dialogue or to understand each other, then there's little hope for us. This nation has been far too divided and partisan for far too long. I don't know what the future will be like, but I only hope that in our eagerness to do what is right that we do not become prey to the temptation of our own self-righteousness.

Rifts

There was a war in heaven when the first idea of disunity came.
Some were elect, others cast down, falling like lightning without rain.

It was bad enough that sin fell into the world to bring death and pain,
But it's even worse now that we suffer in disunity with nothing to gain.

Rifts open, yawning wider than chasms as big as ten Grand Canyons lined up.
Closing them could be easy, would be easier, had people learned to wake up

To the concept of saying *sorry* or owning up to things gone wrong,
But courage is short when victims enjoy playing the violin's song.

Brother against brother, sister against sister, friend against friend,
And no longer can people dream of happy endings without end.

Husband against wife, parents against children, family against family,
And we are left in the dust, carrying on, pretending that we are happy.

We have allowed our feelings to be the judge, jury, prosecutor, and executioner,

When many feelings run free like criminals in a city
without a commissioner.

When has saying, "I'm sorry," ever been an impossible
plank to remove
From eyes, ears, and even mouths when technology is
fast on the move?

We are not evolved, but we have devolved, worse than
animals at times,
Shadows of ourselves in nightmares and demons
drawing dreams of end times.

Wake up all you sleepers! Wake up all you dreamers!
And make real the unthinkable,
Which is a dream of reconciliation where the only thing
that dies is pride unsinkable.

Give in to freedom beyond the prison of your own selfish
view,
And give repentance an honest chance to have your heart
be renewed.

The truth will set you free, even when it hurts and even
when it burns,
Because it's either that or the delusion that grace is
something to be earned.

Autoimmune

An Asian woman was attacked on her way to church in broad daylight.

She was 65 years old.

Supposedly, while she was knocked down, the assailant screamed racist comments at her. I would have imagined she was too dazed on that cold pavement to fully grasp what was happening.

The attack happened around 11:40 a.m. at the 300 block of West 43rd Street, Hell's Kitchen, Manhattan.

Security footage from inside the lobby of a luxury apartment captured it. It also captured lobby staff who were inside watching it all as it happened.

When has anyone ever realized how little good it does when Americans attack other Americans for a race that they were born with? Unlike other countries that are defined as a nation, culture, and race, America is one of the few that is a nation and a culture, but not a race. Race should never have been a factor (though unfortunately, it has in the past). And yet, especially in 2020 and 2021, a virus has made some Americans think that Asians are part of that virus.

Like a body's immune system attacking itself because of something broken inside of it, we Americans have become victims of an autoimmune response that's killing the body of our own nation.

But this has always been an issue, with or without a virus.

Some have spoken out against racism, even calling for the end of "white privilege" and referring to white people as "oppressors."

But the man who attacked that woman was black.

Is racism a race thing or a human thing?

Autoimmune diseases can happen to any person, regardless of race. When will the day come when we stop attacking each other using the excuse of biology?

Let Me/Let Us

Let me have this moment to be myself
Away from the crowd,
With you and me, face to face.
No need to pretend, but instead,
Let's both be honest in this time, at this moment,
In this sacred space.

Let us have these words
That are too truthful but not too angry,
That are not poetic and not too wordy,
So that we can air out our dirty laundry.

Let me look at you the way you truly are
And I want you to do the same with me
If we are to untangle this maze of baggage
And get rid of the skeletons that should never be.

Let us work the good work,
Climb the good climb and summit.
For there is a mountain between us,
And the only other option is to plummet.

There is only one absolute truth,
And both of us have pieces of it.
So opening our minds and holding them up,
Let's put these pieces together and recognize it.

Saint Gregor and the Young Prince

There was once a young prince racked with sorrow and anger. So desperate was he to find inner peace that he traveled far into the desert to search for a holy man rumored to know the answers to nearly all questions.

By the time the man came to this hermit's cave, the sun had already set. Outside of the cave's mouth, the holy man had already prepared a fire, complete with a meager supper, just big enough for the both of them. The young man was surprised; he had not told anyone else that he was coming to see the holy man. But the holy man had even already prepared a seat for him.

With a gentle nod of approval, the holy man invited the prince to sit across from him and to accept a porridge of lentils, fragrant herbs, and nuts.

It wasn't long after eating that the young man couldn't wait another moment to plead his case.

"Father Gregor, many have told me that you have answers," declared the young man, the last bite of food not even fully down his gullet. "Please, help me find peace. I feel hurt all the time. I sleep and dream only of the wrong that others have done to me. I can't help but feel angry. What should I do?"

Father Gregor, the holy man, sought by many, shifted his wise gaze from the fire he tended and, with his dark eyes, settled upon the man. He then spoke in a patient and compassionate tone, his seraphic face in perfect calm.

"Stop being God."

The prince was puzzled. What did Father Gregor mean by this? He never considered himself to be God. He did, however, believe in Him. The young man knew that he was obviously far from being any type of god.

"Sir . . ." the young man paused for a moment placing down his empty bowl. "I appreciate your hospitality, but what you said does little to help me. I think you fail to see my problem. I came to find answers, and yet you give me nothing that I wanted; if anything, there is now more mystery. Please, tell me what I should do with my life."

The old man, his beard weathered by the aged desert winds, simply opened his mouth once more and said, "Stop being God."

Frustrated, the young man's features began to flush as he felt that he had come here for naught. He had spent days traveling through harsh terrain simply to get to Father Gregor. The locals were of little to no use to him because they seemed to be quite an uneducated folk, so pleading with them was barely worth the bother.

"What game are you playing with me, old man?! Are you but a charlatan, out to thrift me of my time and patience? In my own land, no one would dare waste my time, let alone my patience. My servants, who number in the hundreds, would not even think to cross me even in my better days!"

Throughout this prince's rant, Father Gregor stayed as composed as the soft desert wind; its cool night touch caressed the gray of his long hair, aged by years of prayer and contemplation. He simply stared at the young man as the prince eventually came to the end of his rant.

"... I would have you know that those who crossed me had much to regret, and though you are a man of the cloth, who do you have to protect you?"

But as the young man spoke this, the last of his rage simmered out, and he almost immediately regretted his last sentence. Catching his tongue, he closed his eyes for a moment to compose himself before placing a hand over his eyes in shame.

"... I'm-I'm sorry ... I've gotten so used to being angry that I forget whom I'm talking to ... please ... Father Gregor ... please forgive me."

The old man, seeing the remorse of the young ruler, allowed a swell of compassion to beam over his weather-worn features as his lips spoke absolution.

"Do not worry, young man. The blood of Christ covers you."

Brushing back his black curly locks, the young ruler sighed in momentary relief before speaking again.

"Sir ... I just wish that you would explain to me why you keep saying that I am God or I am being God, when it's clear to both of us that this is not the case."

The ruler waited for a moment in a pause, expecting Father Gregor to answer. But the old man remained silent. The ruler hesitated a moment but then spoke again.

"Please, good sir, I beg you for clarity."

The old man, satisfied with the eagerness of this ruler to humble himself, then finally spoke as the fire between them illuminated their features in the desert night.

"Whenever you think only of what makes you happy, regardless of the welfare of others, you are making yourself God. Whenever you think that you are entitled to anything and that nothing is given to you by grace, then you are being God to yourself. When you think that your time is more valuable than anyone else's, you are being God to yourself. Whenever you withhold forgiveness and mercy to those who wronged you or to those who've failed your standard, then you are being God to yourself. But you, my son, are not God."

The ruler's eyes blinked for a moment as a realization came over him.

"It is God alone who loves unconditionally, perfectly, and selflessly. It is God who forgives us regardless of how often or how far we fail. It is God who alone deserves all glory and worship simply because of who He is. When we seek to place ourselves as God in our sinfulness; as God in our selfishness, we bring only misery, hatred, and vanity into our lives. Go and love like God. Go and forgive like God. Go and bless others like God. But do not seek to place yourself as God, for you are a man, and it is you who needs Him, not the reverse. So then, stop being Him."

The young ruler was silent and speechless. For the next three days and three nights, the prince fasted, confessing his sins to God, before joining the hermit in a final meal. After reciting the Lord's prayer, the prince headed home. On his journey back he had found the locals who he had first neglected and joined them in a meal, giving alms to them as he later continued on his way.

From that day forth, upon returning, the prince ruled his lands with justice and mercy, finally finding a peace in his heart that he had never known: one that surpassed all understanding.

Message to Self, May 12, 2021: It's Not That Bad

I'm worried about a work meeting this Thursday because I have to present an update on a brief section.
Meanwhile, India is burning bodies each day as swaths of their people die from COVID.
That meeting isn't as bad as you think.

I'm uncomfortable about having a family Zoom meeting Saturday morning.
I really wanted to have my morning free, but it looks like that's not happening.
Meanwhile, Israelis and Palestinians are attacking each other, launching rockets from both sides, hitting buildings and killing people.
Attending a Zoom meeting from your bedroom isn't as bad as you make it.

I'm angry that I feel bored at work, and even when I tell my boss that I'm free, I'm stuck doing boring listings that I don't want to do.
Meanwhile, thousands of unemployed Americans line up to get food just to feed themselves and their families, even for one more lousy week.
Being bored at your job isn't that bad at all.

A World of Darkness and Light

Written 5/16/21

Late last week, the CDC announced that face masks were no longer required for those who were vaccinated when they enter crowded places outdoors and for most indoor settings (with exceptions for places like health-care settings). Currently, 56.7% of the US population has received a vaccination shot, and cases have been declining throughout the country as certain states, including NJ, will open up to almost full capacity by next week. The time I'm writing this is Sunday, May 16, 2021. The sun is out, and though it was forecasted to be a cloudy day, it still appears to be a beautiful day nonetheless.

Meanwhile, in the past several weeks, India has suffered over 23 million COVID cases and has seen over 250,000 deaths. They have been suffering from oxygen shortages, a new COVID variant, and recent reports of the appearance of a "black fungus" that occurs in their COVID patients.

Also, violence has erupted between Israel and Palestine, as rockets and airstrikes have been exchanged between both sides. This eruption happened supposedly in response to Israel's threat to evict Palestinian families and from police restrictions placed on Muslims' celebrating Ramadan.

Things are getting better (though not perfect) in the US, whereas other parts of the world burn. But in human history, this has always been the case in some form. Prosperity and plague have constantly coexisted in this world, fluctuating and changing with the passage of time. In the past few days, I have spent time thinking about this. And with everything that's been going on, I can't help but feel some degree of "survivor's guilt," at least in light of how quickly things are returning to normal where I am while bad things are happening in other parts of the world. But what, then, are the options?

I could, instead of finding contentment in the good of things, focus on the anger and the sadness of the other things that are going on. I could, for instance, spend time contemplating on how unfair human existence is and even spend hours ruminating on the cursed existence of humanity. But what good would come out of this, especially when there is little to nothing that can be done about what's happening: namely, with more complicated and entangled issues such as the Israeli–Palestinian conflict? Obsessing only on the evils of this world, out of guilt, is not a solution when no solution is accessible to any one person. There will always be evil and suffering in this world, regardless of timing. Humanity is fallen, and there shouldn't be any surprise that suffering is the price that comes with it. And if a person resolves to never be happy until there is no evil in the world, that would be purely delusional and, in all cases, impractical.

But at the same time, the other extreme would not be favorable either, where one embraces an almost toxic positivity, a mindset that utterly ignores the suffering of the world and focuses only on avoiding any mention of it whatsoever in favor of a self-contained bubble. And even in that bubble, one can then take the further step of also avoiding any personal suffering, even at the neglect of helping others and loved ones.

What then do we make of this situation? We live in a world of light and darkness. And as much as there will always be darkness in the world, one cannot deny that there are still good things too and that good things can still happen. But how should we live our lives according to this paradox?

I've thought about this. And personally, I do struggle with this, even now, to some degree. Whenever there is the idea of tremendous suffering coexisting with tremendous privilege, there are no easy answers. Compared with so many others and the majority of the world, I live in tremendous privilege. I was born in a fully developed country that is not war-torn and is prosperous in many ways; I have freedoms that many people in other countries do not have. I have been blessed with being raised in a loving family that, although not perfect, were well off and did not struggle in the ways many other families in the world have struggled. I will not hide from that. I have been given and privileged with vastly more than I deserve.

At where I am in my life and based on what I know, I believe that the most practical solution in light of this dilemma, in light of this struggle of living in a world of darkness and light, is to live life as responsibly and as morally as I can for myself and for others. This will also include living as one who is informed and aware of the struggles going on in other parts of the world. Now bear in mind that a line should be drawn in terms of how deeply informed one should be about these matters because when it comes to knowledge, one can delve as deeply or as shallowly as they choose. In my years of living, especially when it comes to politics, one can go very deep into a rabbit hole and get caught up into partisanship to a level where they can blind themselves to obvious things. In such cases, balance and objectivity should be kept in mind.

I'm happy that things are returning to normal in America. I'm happy that today appears to be sunnier than forecasted. I'm happy that I have most of this day to myself to rest, relax, and recover before heading back to another work week. But at the same time, I allow myself to be upset and saddened by the tragedy of what is happening in India and the Middle East. These tragedies do not falter my faith in God because this is something God made clear in His Scripture about the brokenness of mankind and the world mankind had chosen to live in. I pray that these tragedies will be remedied sooner rather than later and trust that God is still in control even when I am not. I accept that I don't have answers to these evils, and I don't think, as I mentioned before, that any one person on earth has the answer. But amid it all, I choose to allow myself to be happy with what has been given to me, even if I don't deserve it. I choose to be thankful with all that I've been blessed with. And I choose to live morally and respectfully, not just for the sake of myself and my loved ones but also for the sake of those who are not as fortunate as me. That is the least I can do.

The Sound of Rain

If every moment of my life fell like drops of rain,
Would I be foolish to try to catch each drop,
Cupping my hands like a madman
As though losing every gold coin he had
From the sky?

If I were to focus only on the measly amount
My frail palms can gather,
Would I not miss the landscape,
The trees, the fields, and all things that were
Influenced by every drop captured or not?

Many men,
Many women,
Many, many people
Dash to and fro
"Selfie-ing," posting, envying,
And comparing their filled hands with each other
Before time and gravity take everything away.

I have been like them for too long.
Too long. Too frequently. Too wasteful.

The rain falls both on the wicked and on the righteous,
And how it is used, how it is harnessed
Is of one's own choosing.

I do not know the secrets of the world
Nor the mysteries or anatomy of the weather.
But I think I will choose to no longer hoard.

The Problem of Endless Ambition

There will never be enough.

There will always be more to do.

There will always be something you don't have.

There will always be more to expect.

There will always be bad that will happen.

There will always be not enough good done.

There will always be more that should have been said.

There will always be someone better than you.

There will always be someone higher than you.

There will always be something missing.

There will always be too much or too little.

You will never be enough.

You will never have enough.

You will never succeed at everything.

You will never know enough.

You will never own enough.

You will never be honored enough.

You will never be loved enough.

You will always find something wrong.

You will never be done.

The Solution of "But"

But unless you're dying, you already have enough.

But even though there is always more to do, there is always more to be thankful for.

But even though you don't have everything, you don't need everything.

But don't always expect that you deserve more.

But there will always be good that will happen.

But don't stop doing good.

But sometimes silence is enough.

But be better for your sake and not for comparison.

But be thankful that there is someone or something higher than you.

But isn't this the human condition?

But there is always such a thing as enough.

But you are loved anyway.

But you have more than you deserve.

But succeeding in everything doesn't teach you everything.

But was it ever our place to know everything?

But how do you define "enough"?

But it's an honor just to be alive.

But you are loved and do not realize this.

But you can always find something right.

But "never" can be a subjective word.

Mid-Life ~~Crisis~~ Growth

Written 6/2/21

It's a day before my 43rd birthday, June 2, 2021. It seems eventful but at the same time uneventful because I guess by the time you're middle-aged, birthdays don't have that same exhilaration as they did when you were young. I'm not fully sure exactly how to feel about this, other than to accept it as it is. But one thing I can ask myself is the following: what exactly have I learned, now that I'm halfway down the road (so to speak)? Well, I think asking that question is a good way to start.

1. The key to life isn't happiness, it's meaning.
It's not enough to pursue happiness in life. Happiness comes and goes and can be influenced and torn down by so many things. And when you do get the things that you believe will make you happy, it's only a matter of time before you get bored of them and need to find something new. The fresh appeal of a new thing fades. The romance of a new relationship becomes routine. And the thrill of a new fad fades away the moment when that new fad becomes old. And the cycle continues.

Life should be about the pursuit of meaning and not about how you feel. Having meaning and having a mission in life (provided that the meaning chosen is moral and is something beyond just yourself) does not change, regardless of how good or how bad things get, especially when one fully commits oneself to it.

Take a look at all the great figures in history, whether it be Martin Luther King Jr., Mother Teresa, or even Jesus's Apostles, and ask yourself whether the priority they made in their life was the sole pursuit of their own happiness or for greater meaning? The answer is obvious, especially in light of the suffering (and sometimes even a vicious death) that they were willing to endure to accomplish their goals.

One of the best things about purpose and meaning is that it keeps you focused and that sometimes, when pursuing it, happiness may be found along the way.

2. Being hard on someone doesn't mean that the lesson you're trying to teach them is wrong. Not being hard on someone when you need to be isn't loving them either but hurting them.

There are plenty of times in my life when I hated the people who corrected me harshly or reprimanded me for things that I'd messed up on. But when I look back on those moments and what I've learned from those mistakes, sometimes I wish I could go back and thank them. Now of course, this doesn't justify harshness simply for the sake of it, and there's a line that can be crossed when harshness becomes bullying and abuse, but remember, just because someone else is hard on you, it doesn't mean the lesson they're trying to teach you is wrong. And in some cases, I've seen when people should have been strict with others when they needed a swift kick in the behind hold back from giving it. And I've seen the consequences. It's even worse when you're the one who needed that swift kick in the behind but didn't get it, and others suffer as a consequence.

3. Building wealth, possessions, and networks are meaningless without building character.

It's better to die a good man, alone and poor, than die a villain surrounded by fake friends and wealth achieved through immoral means.

Your body fades, your mind goes, and your energy decreases as you age. But the things that do not necessarily fade with time (or at least are more lasting), provided that you spent your lifetime building them up, are your virtue, your honesty, your discipline, your kindness, your wisdom, and your courage.

Just as with anything, character has to be exercised; it needs to be applied day in and day out with minor things and especially with major ones. It's an investment, and it needs to be practiced in your relationships, your job, your time off, your errands, and every other aspect of your life. Whether it means showing kindness to your coworkers (even though at times they irritate you) or being disciplined about getting your errands done on time and done well, character is essential.

But remember, it requires work. Because at the end of the day, buying things or spending money on an extravagant vacation is easy, but working on yourself is almost always difficult but worth it in the end because of the difference it will make in your life and in the lives of those you affect, which will be lasting.

4. Balance and moderation should be applied to almost everything.

Well, first off, what is balance? The closest definition I can come up with, in this case, would be the amount of resources (time, energy, focus, etc.) you can pour into something before it starts interfering with other essential aspects of your life.

As you grow older, you realize that there's only so much time and energy a person has each day, and that you can't do everything. The sooner one accepts that, the sooner they can start prioritizing and realizing that some things may not be as essential as they once thought they were.

But of course, there's a right way and a wrong way to prioritize. In this case, once an aspect of your life starts detracting greatly from your higher priorities, you need to have the courage to ask yourself, even if you don't want to, whether that thing you're pouring so much into is even worth having or worth investing in.

I have heard many horror stories of people who sacrifice their family for work, and I have seen the results, in one way or another. And as much as many others have heard those same stories, does it make sense that sometimes, even though we know them, that we still fall victim to becoming just like them?

5. Tragedy happens to everyone. The way you respond to it determines whether it builds you up or tears you down.

Life is suffering. It's a simple truth. And though suffering happens more to some and less to others, suffering is inescapable. The best we can do is to try to minimize it by being careful and aware. But despite all of our plans, tragedy hits everyone regardless of their walk of life. So instead of being unrealistic by trying to avoid all tragedy in life, accept the fact that tragedy is a part of it. But remember, too, that even though circumstances can be uncontrollable, the one thing you can control is yourself — specifically, how you respond to those circumstances. Choosing to respond to something the right way can build you up and cause you to grow, even when such a thought may seem impossible at the time. But you do have more control over your responses than you think. That leads me to my next point.

6. When tragedy builds you up, go out and pay it forward.

Several years ago, at my workplace, I remember this one young girl who was upset with her life at the moment. I did spend time talking to her about it, and it seemed that she felt stressed about her life and dissatisfied with her work; though that isn't necessarily a life crisis, to her it was a big thing. One of the things we spoke about was religious belief.

Being Christian, I inevitably brought up the truth about repentance to God. One of the things that the girl said in reply was that she was repentant to God, so why wouldn't God just take her out of the world, since she's right with Him. Based on our conversation, she obviously wasn't wishing that God would strike her down and bring her to heaven, but it seemed more that she wanted God to just teleport her right out of this world and straight into paradise.

At the time, when I was younger, I didn't really have a direct answer to give her, possibly because it was such a theoretical scenario. But over time, the more I thought about it, the more I realized another reason why God just doesn't rapture people up to heaven the moment they accept Him. God keeps us here so that we can help others who are in need.

When you have faced your tragedy and grown from it, use those lessons you've learned to help others. In doing so, not only will you find the meaning behind why something has happened to you, but you can help others find their meaning in turn. It also helps you build character, which is an invaluable investment because that investment is you.

7. Admitting that you're wrong and saying you're sorry is not the end of the world. In fact, many times, it makes the world more right. But just be sure you're apologizing for the right thing.

No one likes being wrong. But honestly, as much as this is an overly mentioned notion in many self-help books and articles, there's a good reason for it. I have seen example after example of people refusing to admit that they're wrong and the devastation that this causes, in the people I love, in my own life, and in the lives of others. You may not like being wrong, but staying wrong without apology actually makes it worse. Really, sometimes it just becomes an issue of suffering a little now or suffering a lot more later on. Save yourself the trouble.

But also be careful that you make sure that you're apologizing for and admitting that you're wrong about the right things. Because if you end up apologizing for the wrong things, that becomes enabling to the other person, who may actually need a swift kick in the pants so they won't end up hurting themselves or others later on with their wrong views.

But then, how do you know what to apologize for if you're in a circumstance when things are not clear? Well, that leads me to my next point.

8. Asking for help does not mean you're weak. In fact, it's quite the opposite, in many cases.

Let's be clear, you're not perfect. You know that. Everyone knows that. You cannot do everything. Ditto. But why do some people prefer to do things alone, the wrong way, until the very final moment of crisis, before asking for help? The easy answers are pride, the fear of shame, the fear of looking weak, etc. But sometimes, getting the job done right the first time around, with others helping, is much better than not getting the job done at all, or done horribly, by doing it all alone.

9. Careless comments and careless actions can come back to haunt you. So be careful, even when you don't think others are listening or looking.

I have done many things I've regretted. And apart from a few exceptions, many of them fall into the category of things I thought weren't a big deal at the time but later on turned out to have affected people much more than I wanted to. Often, people do not purposefully, without reason, cause major catastrophes with their eyes wide open. In fact, if anything, most disasters caused by people result from the sum of small, overlooked choices, building up over days, months, or even years. In fact, sometimes, it's the casual comments or the things that you say without concern that can hurt others the most, even when you don't realize what you're saying. Make no mistake, everything you do is important, regardless of what some people may say. Find this out the easy way now, or go the hard way and regret it later.

10. There's a reason why being a fulltime lone-ranger Christian doesn't work.

Inevitably, as a Christian, my faith has been the center of my life, and because of that, it's due time to bring it up in full steam. I won't be afraid or ashamed to admit that. And for many years, I would hear it said that you should not be a "lone-ranger Christian," as in, a Christian who goes at things alone and is not connected to a community.

You can't do life alone, and there's a reason for this. Having others in your life, ideally those who are pursuing the same values as you, helps you with everything listed above, and some of the things listed above may not even be achievable without others who have your best interests at heart. This is not to say that you can't have moments where you have to take care of something alone (because, trust me, there will be plenty of opportunities for that). But it is to say that sometimes, the greatest good can only be achieved in a community of people all striving for the same good.

For those of you who are not Christian and who are reading this, this point of finding and investing in a loving community is equally important, regardless of your ideological bent. You see, growing up, I actually wanted to be away from people. I hated people, in fact. People were the ones who bullied me and rejected me when I was growing up. Originally, I studied to become an environmental scientist in the hopes that I could find a job "among the trees" and away from people. But the older and older I got, the more I realized that people need people, namely the right people, even though at times a person may doubt that. It's hard to trust anyone, with the way things are going, and I get that. But believe me, ever since I found a home in a community of friends willing to go the extra mile to help each other, that has helped me to do the same for them, no matter how bad things get.

Just the other day, after getting a haircut, I noticed how more evident my gray hairs were on my head. Looking in the mirror, especially if I spent more time than the usual glance, I could see the imperfections on my face: the wrinkles, the wear lines, all the signs of being an older man who is not as sharp, not as youthful, and not as "vibrant" as he once was. But that was pretty much the same as last year or even the year before that. Age is what it is. It's an aspect of life, and growing old is what it is. From what I know and what I have seen in my life, being middle-aged is not a crisis as long as you focus on the things that matter rather than on the things that don't. In truth, it's just like any other age; it has its unique challenges and its unique benefits, but it's not a deal breaker. It is what you make of it, and I'm not suggesting constantly pretending that you're young again when you're not, while ignoring all the responsibilities that you have. It's remembering that each day is a gift and not an entitlement, and that sometimes, if not all the time, life really isn't just about you. It's about something far greater. And realizing that matters more than you can imagine.

Master Thyself

When I was young, I wanted to slay dragons and have cool powers.
But then I realized that dragons that breathed fire weren't real and that I barely even survived middle school gym class.

When I was young, I wanted to be an astronaut.
But then I saw the *Challenger* accident and stopped wanting to be that.

When I was young, I wanted to work for the environment, to work among the trees, and to have no one bother me.
But then I went to college and discovered that working for the environment led you to the dirtiest places, and not the ones that were already clean.

When I was young, I couldn't wait to be on my own and move out of my parents' house. But then I actually moved, and I realized that being on your own wasn't as exciting as I imagined.

When I was young, I wanted to have a lot of money to feel safe and secure and to buy anything. But then I got a lot of money, and I still didn't feel totally safe or secure.

And then one day I met a man who finally told me what I needed to hear, but didn't want to listen to at the time.

He said, "Seek not to always change your circumstances, for circumstances are fickle and mostly uncontrollable. Change yourself instead, and then things will follow."

I'm older now, and I still don't have cool powers.
But now there *are* dragons that I can slay (even if they don't breathe fire).

I'm older now, and though I don't have that dream job, I know that greatness begins when one realizes that there's no such thing as accidents.

I'm older now, and I get involved in messes that always need to be cleaned up.
But there's nothing more rewarding than making that which was wrong right again.

I'm older now, and I still live on my own.
But now I see something more than excitement: I see accomplishment.

I'm older now and I have found something worth more than money: blessing those who I love with it.

Alone on a Poconos Deck

Near summer has come, and I am here idle,
Having some peace in a deck chair's cradle.

In a time away with friends but now by my lonesome,
On a day with sunlight, trees, and all birds handsome,

I do not wish to think or overthink any labor that I have,
As a tense madman stands with a taskmaster's staff.

The day is slow but fast as leisure days are meant;
Not to be rushed nor declared but wisely spent.

You who read, do not take lightly the need for leisure, be
you busy or not,
Since God Himself, busy as He is, rested even when He
needed it not.

The Dog Days of Summer 2021

Today, we choose to fill with laughter, with candles, and fire pits where amber-lit faces share family bonds without bloodlines to trace.

Today, we choose to fill with iced drinks and memories fading in on polaroid photos taken fresh from still life moments.

Today, we choose to dine outdoors and indoors, if needed, when the mosquitoes bite or when a much-needed AC blows.

Today, we coin new nicknames, not in mocking but in friendship, where inside jokes are hidden avenues leading to encouragement.

Today, we will not venture into the dark news of nowadays, yesterdays, or days to come.

Today, we will fill instead with moments shaped by spaces of tranquility, outdoor barbeques, and noticing each time the sun shines through clouds that cannot tame its rays.

Today, we will define as part of our golden years even when we are not too old and still too young (wrinkles or not).

Today, we choose to live and live in the light of what is now — the nowness of joy, the nowness of friends, the nowness of family, and the nowness of summer.

Today, we choose life in the face of darkness and in the face of light.

Today, we choose life.

Simply

Why must it be so hard to live simply?

To simply enjoy simplicity without being complicated?

Are we so habitually lost in our workaholic guilt as to feel that we've sinned when we do nothing?

Are we so fixed on flogging ourselves like pain-filled penitents if we define achievement by stating, "I simply relaxed today"?

There is a cruel god with an unmarked altar.

Where it is can depend on who you are.

It's larger and more pronounced in some cultures.

This god goes by many names: hustling, productivity, and in some cases, the sense of self-worth.

Stop feeding this god with your vain sacrifices. This god was never meant to be.

Stop and look around you and know that toil when not needed is a curse.

Stop and realize counterfeit work from the genuine blessing.

Stop and love, but please, know that loving oneself isn't always ego gone astray.

Stop and eat from every tree that the true God has given you to eat from, but eat not from the tree of the knowledge of productivity and consumerism.

Stop and be free. Know that life can be found in solitude and stillness and the simplest of joys.

God has given you this day your daily bread, but it means little if you don't live today but only in a series of unwritten tomorrows.

The Outcast God

They always talk behind Your back like You can't hear them or like You're too distant to care.

But You hear them all of the time — taking Your name in vain, cursing You, blaming You, and treating You like a useless piece of crap.

They say that they hate You in more than just words and even go so far as to accuse You of being dead. They might as well just say to Your face that You're dead to them.

When You intervene, they may thank You (though many times they don't), only to turn around and forget that You're even there. Or they treat You as a genie — loving You one moment and turning on You the next, just because You failed to grant them their wishes.

But the worst thing happens when You intervene or say something to help them, and they treat You as the bad guy. They accuse You of being too controlling — that You're unfair, that You're too demanding, or that You're too strict.

Most of it's out of line because they have false expectations of You. But sometimes it's because of others who claim to speak for You but don't and mislead many into thinking that You're that way, when You're not.

And when You don't intervene, they then blame You for being an absentee Father at best and at worst someone who's full of crap and a righteous uncaring tyrant.

To add insult to injury, anyone who follows You, the world turns its back on them and hates them just because of You.

They may even hate them enough to kill them, either because they deliver something others don't want to hear or just . . . just because.

And just because You don't give people what they want the way they want it or just because You don't jump through the hoops that they expect You to, then You become the bad guy and everyone then blames You for the mess that others (or they) have caused.

It's as though anything You do is not enough for them, even though You could easily will them out of existence.

But still You cling to the world's existence, holding the universe like a burning dumpster fire, preventing it from falling further when the easiest thing You could do is to let go — to let it all fall and spiral into nothingness. No more cruelty. No more stupidity. No more mockery of who You are.

But You are the God of everything.

The Alpha and Omega.

The God who died a spat-upon martyr for a world that didn't deserve You.

But, more so, You are the God of outcasts, because it seems often that the outcasts are the ones who realize how much they need You.

Beyond time, You sit on Your throne a servant king, aching for a world too deaf to hear and too self-absorbed to listen, and in the madness of it all, You still love them.

The Desperate Hosanna

Save me from myself, Lord, for the spirit is unwilling and my flesh is weak.

I cannot stand to live in my hopelessness.

My mind is my Judas; my horrible habits fetters of tyranny.

I stand unbearably breathing while I cower in my own oppression.

For I have become my own master and, in doing so, have become my own slave.

Save me from myself, Lord, because I seek only the convenience of myself,

Convenience having become so much a curse when at first I believed was a blessing.

I have abused You. I have abused others.

And because I've done both, I have abused myself.

What wretchedness there is in the love of only Self!

For it is a god who is not God and whose worship is a vacant path leading only to loathing.

Save me from myself, Lord, because the love only of Self isn't love at all

When friends and family fall by the wayside, drowning in their desperation.

I am a wretch filled with sin, and I long for reconciliation,

Only to keep choosing the opposite.

Do not leave me here to die when You are the way, the truth, and the resurrection.

My only hope is You, the real I AM, who I believe in and not the "I am" in the mirror.

Save me from myself, Lord, because I have a blind spot shaped in my image.

My will is bent and distorted by years of only caring, pitying, and wanting myself.

Liberate the slave that I call ego. Emancipate the prisoner I call wretchedness.

Name them anew, because freedom without a name is wisdom without awe.

You are my hope. You *are* my hope. And I refuse to stop wanting You.

A Perspective on Worship

Written 8/8/21

Growing up in a Christian household and going to church nearly every Sunday, I always had a view ingrained into me of what it means to worship God. You stand when they tell you to. You sing from a book or from words posted on a screen. You try your best not to sound tone deaf (though I'm pretty sure I failed at this part many times). And you make sure you try to mean it. The last part wasn't so much specifically instructed as it was implied.

Now, older and middle-aged, some of that view has broadened a bit. Now it also includes listening to Christian music a lot on the radio. But then again, if the song isn't your "thing," you either find another station or you download another Christian song that "fits" your taste more.

And all the while, through my many years of being a Christian, arguments or sentiments here and there rise up between congregations. Worship with drums is sinful. Worship should only be with the classics and not with all those "rock and roll" songs because those are worldly. Or on the flip side, churches who say that worship with drums is sinful or who discourage contemporary music are legalistic and judgmental. When I look at these arguments, I feel that many Christians may be missing the point of worship in general.

Because the question is this: Why do we need to worship God at all? Is it as though God actually needs our worship, and if He doesn't get it, would His power diminish? Well, no to the last point, and that goes without saying (how would He have the power to create the angels and the universe before there was anyone to worship Him?).

When I initially think about these questions, there's almost a knee-jerk reaction about it. Is God really so narcissistic that He desperately wants our worship? If we don't worship Him, would that be an offense to Him? Of course, having these thoughts almost always triggers a guilt thing for having them, but I think these questions need to be asked. In truth, there's something about the natural human heart that causes us to be repulsed by the idea of "worshipping" something or someone.

And that's when I realize the irony of this sentiment. Why do most people seem to have a disdain toward the idea of "worship," especially if they are not religious, and yet how is it so natural that every human eventually ends up worshipping something in their life? It doesn't have to be God. And that worship doesn't have to be with praise songs. You could worship money by just focusing your entire life on getting more of it. You could worship relationships simply by sacrificing everything you have just to obtain some ideal of it. And most of all, you could even end up worshipping yourself, even at the cost of hurting whoever you need to hurt and stepping on whoever you need to step on to get ahead.

Humanity is a species of worship. Being human automatically comes with the need to be a part of something greater than ourselves. Being Homo sapiens comes with the need to find meaning in things, regardless of how aware we are of it or not. If that wasn't the case, why do people seek solace in the transcendent? Why do people show reverence for art, music, and stories that inspire them to become better versions of themselves, even when such things are not needed for basic survival?

So, in hindsight, is it really all that bad that God would want us to direct ourselves to Him, the highest representation of good, given that He already knows that all the other options tend not to be better or, at worst, self-destructive?

Also, if God was such a narcissist and would only give attention to those who first praised Him, why then would He love us first when we really didn't know Him and were His enemies, even to the point of allowing Himself to be killed by us (Romans 5:8)?

But maybe He sacrificed His Son as a preemptive measure to force us to love Him back. Maybe that's why He did it. But then this argument fails because even after the fact, God still leaves people the option to walk away from Him, even though He has the power to will us to do anything.

In the end, the picture of God comes more into focus when we realize the truth of who we are and the truth of what He's done, even when He didn't need us.

If anything, worship seems more to be for us than for Him, even if what it does is simply remind us of who we are as creatures and where He stands in what He's given us: gifts that we do not deserve.

I look back at my life and remember all of the times my family or my friends or my pastor have helped me tremendously or have given me something far beyond what I deserve. Just this past year, as a birthday gift, a bunch of my close friends came together and subsidized a portion of a trip to Ireland that I wanted to take. In fact, the actual story behind it is that my pastor, who I consider a close friend, spoke to me in earnest about not being afraid to ask for a gift even though I was fine with not getting a gift at all for my birthday. He actually pushed for it. And when I found out the willingness of my friends to chip in a hefty sum, I felt so grateful and blown away by it that I wrote all of them a sincere email expressing my thankfulness.

This wasn't the only case of when I expressed how grateful I was to the people in my life. I remember how often my pastor sacrificed his time, his energy, and his effort to help me through many crises that happened in my life (some of which were from my own doing) and how little he asked for in return. I remember all of the times my parents loved me, even when I treated them poorly or took them for granted. And throughout these times, I have sent lengthy letters or emails or pricey gifts, thanking the people who I love for what they've given me; gifts that I do not deserve.

But then I look back at my own worship life towards God. I look at how, for so many years, I had a limited picture of worship in my own life: turning on the Christian music station when I drove, reciting what's on the screen at a religious service, superficially saying thank you to God during my prayers without deeply thinking about it. If I went to greater lengths to thank the people in front of me, why has it been so different with God?

If it wasn't for Him, I wouldn't have the friends and family that I have in my life. If it wasn't for Him, I wouldn't have the privileged life that I have now. If it wasn't for Him, I wouldn't have been given the strength and direction to have dealt with the hard things in my life. And if it wasn't for Him, I wouldn't have the promise of heaven, given by His sacrificed Son.

The other thing that worship does is remind us that we need to be grateful. It reminds us that even when times are hard, we have someone who fights harder for us. It reminds us that the being who we worship has things under His control even when there doesn't seem to be any sense of that at all. Because in the end, what is life without a transcendental sense of gratitude? It's absurdity, superficiality, and, in the worst case, entitled cynicism.

In my own life, I haven't been fair to God, and I haven't been as thankful to Him as I have been toward the people around me. And I regret this.

"Father, I know I don't give You the thanks You deserve. I just get so caught up in myself: my own struggles, the things in front of me, and my own insufficiencies. These are not excuses.

I haven't been fair to You, and even though You hear me say "Thank You" to You on occasion, no amount of thanks is ever good enough compared with what You have given me in life.

I just want You to know that I love You, and I appreciate everything You've done. You've always deserved more, and You are the most important being in my life. Help me to actually keep making You more of that every single moment that I breathe.

Each breath is a gift from You. Every good thing is a thing that You allowed me to have that I am not entitled to. None of the worship that I can possibly give can ever be righteous (not even this prayer). But because of Your Son, I can be here, now, righteous before You: clothed in Your own righteousness.

Thank you, God. Thank you, Father. I worship You, and I praise You because You are truly greater than anything or anyone in the universe. In Christ's name, amen"

One Minute at a Time

I have looked into the mirror, and in my hair were strands of white,

Visible to the eye with or without the fluorescent bathroom light.

I ask myself whether I've earned these hairs,

Whether I lived as though I actually cared.

I looked into that mirror and saw wrinkles on my face,

More so when I smiled or frowned in whichever case.

I ask myself whether these were stripes of merit and battle,

Whether I really cared beyond what laziness would have settled.

I looked into the mirror and saw an older man staring back

Not being sure to think of what he gained or what he lacked.

I asked myself whether older age can be something of pride

Or a disappointment to a person who didn't get a free ride.

I looked into the mirror and realized that the decisions were there

To either realize a life truly lived or grow bitter in nihilistic despair.

I ask myself if time was fully gone or if there were any choices really left

Or was old age just a thing to remind us of regret and all goodness theft?

I looked into the mirror and decided what my choices would be

Because I did have a choice: a choice to live with the choice of being free.

I told myself that eternal meaning is more important than fleeting happiness

One minute at a time of choosing less and less to live in my own selfishness.

Resolution

The last American troop withdrew from Afghan soil on August 31, 2021.

There was a snapshot of him in full fatigues boarding a C-17 cargo plane through a night vision lens. His eyes didn't seem to be gazing anywhere. The picture wasn't clear enough to see exactly what he was looking at. And it was hard to tell if he was happy, sad, angry, or relieved.

There is no resolution.

This twenty-year Afghanistan war was just like that in the minds of many. At first, it wasn't hard to put together what it was about. An enemy was designated because of this or that, and soldiers were sent to fight.

But over the years everyone's eyes began to drift, becoming 100-yard stares, looking somewhere but also looking nowhere. It was a snapshot of a fatigued America through a night vision lens.

There is no resolution.

Questions were raised, but answers were vague. Why wasn't there better clarity? Why was the intelligence deeply flawed? Why was there so fast of a collapse when before that felt unlikely?

There is no resolution.

If we stayed, history would have judged us. If we left as we did, *especially as we did*, history would still judge us. If you thought the war was unfounded and were against it, people would judge you. If you thought the war was worth it and needed to happen, people would judge you.

Nothing will bring back the lives of those lost on either side. Nothing will bring back the amputated or blown-off limbs of veterans at home. Nothing may ever fully heal the mental scars too invisible to be seen on either side.

There is no resolution.

No one political party is to blame (though many would disagree).

All that's left is the charred taste of ashes with barely enough to dine on.

Give me liberty. Give me freedom.

But dear God, please, give me the one thing that this world does not have —

Resolution.

Not My Kingdom

I've spent too much time imagining myself a king of my
kingdom when really all that I have was always Yours.
I expected to build my own legend on an Earth that
would pass away when Your legacy is the only thing that
endures.

Help me to remember that life is not about me, that it's
not about the monuments that I build,
But that it's about You sending Your Son to die, a
martyr's mission on top of a dark lonely hill.

I've stolen too much time thinking and pondering
how important I'll be to strangers that I don't know,
When You're the one who gives when no one deserves
and reaps when no one cares to sow.

I'm a mess, Father, trying to be a majesty who thinks he's
made of gold when he stands on feet of clay,
While you're the one who crafted diamonds in His mind
long before the very earth was made.

It's about Your kingdom, where even the lowest of low
can be crowned to be the greatest of the first.
It's not about my own kingdom, so teach me now that
You should be the only thing that I thirst.

Render to Caesar

Written 8/16/21

The COVID vaccine has been out and is now accessible to all Americans for the past several months. Vaccine commercials and campaigns are being broadcast nationwide to get people vaccinated to prevent further spread of the virus. In fact, certain states have even offered incentives to get vaccinated by giving people everything from discounted concert tickets to straight-out money. The vaccine supply has been accommodated with little to no shortages everywhere in the US. Yet still the proportion of Americans vaccinated with at least a single shot is still only around 60%.

It's mid-August, and the strain, which initially began in India, called the Delta variant, is now the dominant strain in the US, with hospitalizations surging tremendously throughout the country. Those in the hospital with COVID are overwhelmingly the unvaccinated. It's gotten to the point where mask mandates have been instituted in various states, and various companies are now even requiring their workers to be vaccinated.

America had the opportunity to score a tremendous victory against COVID, but now the country is sliding behind. From what I last checked we still have one of the highest COVID infection rates in the world. And America was the one who developed the vaccines and had perhaps the greatest opportunity to vaccinate everyone.

The saddest thing that troubles me is that one of the most significant populations in America that resist getting the vaccine is that of right-wing evangelical Christians. I did some research on this, and from what I can tell, it appears that a lot of their hesitancy stems from a combination of misinformation, lack of trust in the government, and political biases. And strangely enough, Trump's presidency (which it appears that a lot of this population has high approval of) didn't help because throughout his term he sent many mixed messages about the virus, even calling it a hoax early on.

I consider myself an evangelical Christian. I also even consider myself generally conservative. But in the summer that could have been a celebration of America's and, indirectly, the world's victory over one of the greatest pandemics of our century, has instead become a summer of resurgence and doubt. I'm at a loss for words.

I do believe that people desperately need to get vaccinated if we are ever to reach the end of this disaster. It is a life-or-death situation. But I also believe that it would be wrong for the government to mandate everyone to get vaccinated against their will; this would lead to a violation of civil liberties. I have no solution for this.

But one thing that does come to my mind is how often I see politics being mixed so completely with religion, to the point where it causes more problems than solutions. I actually know an aunt of one of my closest friends who is not only a staunch Republican but also an anti-vaxxer who used to come to my Christian fellowship. And it wasn't that uncommon that, during a discussion, she would interject and suddenly steer the entire message to politics when there wasn't a need to do so. I also remember a pastor from the church that I grew up in having the tendency to not only instill politics into his messages but even to go so far as to incorporate conspiracy theories, to the point where it took away from nearly everything he was preaching about.

I've also seen it indirectly done the other way too, where religion appears to be overshadowed by liberalism, where, despite what the Bible says, political correctness and progressive crusading forced the message to, at best, take a back seat and, at worst, be censored altogether.

When I was young and in college, I was a lot more political than I am now. This shouldn't be a surprise, given that college tends to be a political hotbed for an adolescent finding their identity in the world before adulthood. But ever since then, I've seen leaders, both left and right, put on pedestals only to watch them fall. I have seen claims made by both left and right that show that the concept of "middle ground" and bipartisanship has become as exotic as a nearly extinct species of bird. And I'm tired of it all.

I remember in the book of Matthew, when the Pharisees and the Herodians wanted to trap Jesus by asking him whether they should pay taxes or not, Jesus replied, "Render to Caesar the things that are Caesar's, and to God the things that are God's."

During the past several years, I have made this somewhat of a motto for how I handle religion and politics. It's not to say that Christians can't talk about politics. It's not to say that Christians shouldn't be involved in the political process. In fact, though I'm not perfect at this myself, I do believe that it is every American's responsibility to vote, at the very least in presidential elections. But what I also believe is that when Christians obsess so much about politics to the point where politics define every bit of them, even more so than their identity in Christ, then a line has been crossed. Nowhere in the Bible does it say that being a Christian requires you to be a Republican. Nowhere in the Bible does it say that Jesus was a Democrat. But why, then, do many Christians act so guilty of practicing this?

When Jesus was doing His earthly ministry, He preached what His Father wanted Him to preach. Very little did Jesus go into the complexities of politics, other than referencing how His kingdom is not of this world as well as that one instance mentioned above about Caesar. In fact, it's implied throughout the Gospels that the followers around Him wanted His kingdom to be more political; that He would be the messiah that would overthrow the Roman government and reclaim Israel for its people. But instead, that wasn't Jesus's focus at the time. It wasn't His Father's will for Him to be the political messiah that the masses wanted. It was His will to be the Messiah that everyone (including the gentiles) needed.

And if Christians lose perspective on that and we divide ourselves by political tribalism, won't we become as guilty as the masses were?

Josephine's Choice

It was late morning by the time the sun illuminated the Appalachian hills, their trees showing like fanned brushes of green along the horizon. Josephine found herself struggling to finish cooking the last of the mac & cheese as a feeling of weighted dread crept over her body. What happens if she screws up? She only has one box left, and she didn't want to drive all the way back into town on a Sunday. The store might not be open. She also has to clean her bathroom today. What if something goes wrong? This week was so hard. It was more than what she bargained for.

General anxiety disorder was what they called it when she was diagnosed. It's the constant feeling that everything that can go wrong will go wrong, even when they don't or can't. She had trouble sleeping the previous night, even with over 6 mg of melatonin, which is a little more than what she usually takes. Perhaps she should go back to prescription. No, that would only make things worse. It always does.

As Josephine shakingly lifted a macaroni from the boiling pot, she blew on it hesitantly before quickly putting it into her mouth. It was too soft. She screwed up again. Why can't she ever do anything right? In a short panic, Josephine turned off the fire and quickly drained the boiling pot into the colander she had already set up a half an hour before. Like a wet dead squid, the overcooked pasta slumped into the colander with some of the hot water splashing painfully onto her skin, causing her arms to briefly tense from the pain.

Josephine took in pain. She deserved it after screwing up something as simple as mac and cheese. Why couldn't you ever do anything right you stupid, overweight piece of white trash?

She felt the welling up of tears beneath her strained façade. But she then began to remember what someone at her church told her. "You have a choice, Joey . . . Bad stuff happens to the best of us, big and small . . . but we get to choose . . . and throughout it all, God is love."

But choosing was so hard. With a breath, Josephine then steadied herself, counting down numbers in her mind as she focused her breathing on each count. 10 . . . 9 . . . 8 . . . 7. She was getting there, as she felt herself centering again. It was a grounding technique she'd heard of and, so far, it was working.: 4 . . . 3 . . . 2 . . . 1.

Opening her eyes again, she focused on the landscape outside of her trailer. The sun was still out. The trees on the forested hills still stood regally unperturbed in the September daylight. "The earth will fade away, but the word of the Lord endureth forever . . ."

When the Virgin Mary was told that she would give birth to the Son of God, Josephine wondered whether she ever had panic attacks. Josephine didn't know. But she doubted that Mary would have panicked over soggy mac and cheese. "Cast all of your cares upon Him, for He cares for you...."

Choice was the implied thing here, before one could even do the casting; casting, like the disciple's nets into the sea when Jesus told them to before they received the miracle of the abundant catch. But wouldn't her nets be empty?

Staring at the overboiled pasta in the sink and then out the window above it, Josephine then felt her lips move, as though by instinct, to another verse in her mind, "Choose you this day . . ."

But as the last of the anxiety dripped away from her body a spirit of improv took over, "Choose you this day . . . Josephine . . ."

She needed to go out there. To put herself out there, in the fields, outside of her trailer. Sure, it was scary. Sure, it didn't make sense. And sure, it might not make all of her anxious thoughts go away. But at least it would still be her choice. And if she stayed anxious, it would be better to be anxious outside than trapped and anxious inside.

Putting aside her worn apron, Josephine quickly slipped on her crocs and opened her trailer door, heading out to the field outside.

The sun hit her like a holy anointing of gold and light, shining like an unintentional halo past her face and throughout her body. Its heat welcomed her as the momentary smell of fresh air made her forget all that she had worried about.

Josephine felt free.

By the time her eyes adjusted to the light, the anxious thoughts were more silent as they came back, tip-toeing into her mind like greedy thieves on a mid-sized bank heist. But, at least now, she realized she could say one thing about today.

It was still a sunny day. It was still a beautiful day, perfectly cooked mac and cheese or not.

122

Stretching out her arms as though to give the landscape an embrace, she inhaled the air of the hills, the trees, the azure sky, the grass beneath her, and even the distant highway that wasn't too far from the small town nearby. She had made a choice and, with that, even though she knew that the fearful thoughts would come back in force shortly afterwards, she had at least owned this moment.

She, Josephine, had made a choice instead of not making one at all. And as crazy as it sounded, a spontaneous hallelujah came out of her lips.

"I, Josephine DuBois, choose this day . . . I, Josephine DuBois of Appalachia, choose to be free . . ."

Virtuous Pride

It is not found in the boasts of arrogant men, who beat
their breasts and holler,

But in the calloused hands of hard labor and in the sweat
of a good day's work.

It is not found in the empty speech or threats that
emanate from insecure lungs

But in the sacrifice that beats from the heart of honor and
integrity.

It is not found in fading things, designed to oppress and
pull others down

But in the achievements of those lifted up above oneself
through mentorship.

Pride lies not on the outside, where it can be easily
wounded and is held up by nothing.

It lies within and can endure, wounded or not, when
born from virtue and quality.

Pride glows when one's honest work proves true in
storm and rain

But shines even brighter when it breeds goodness in the
lives of others.

Pride is the harvest that comes out of hard work, sincere
intent, and honed skill

And does not necessarily favor the naturally strong, the
talented, or the entitled.

It is meant to be lived and is a side effect of excellence put into practice.

It is not an excuse for the vain.

It is the evidence of living and working in, working for, and working by the truth.

It is not an excuse covered up by lies.

It is a gift when one does good work,

And with all gifts of virtue, it is meant to inspire.

Listen

Listen to me.

You are far stronger

And way tougher than you think.

You may not feel that way.

You may not think that way.

But you are.

What happened in the past is in the past,

And it doesn't have to be your prison.

There's nothing wrong with admitting that you're weak.

Being vulnerable is in fact being strong.

But there's no excuse for you

To purposefully remain weak

When you can become stronger.

Try, strive, push, fight. You need to carry on.

Your existence is more important to the world

Than you realize.

Do good, love others, choose the right thing,

And prove that you're worth it; because you are.

But those things won't happen if you give up.

There's more at stake than you know

If you let go of that ledge that you're clinging to.

If you can't pull yourself up, then reach out.

It doesn't have to be over,

And you can—no, you will do it.

You will make it.

Beholden

Let us tarry as the November days grow short.

Let us feel the crunch of crisp leaves beneath our feet.

Let us gaze at the colored tree line flushed with golds, reds, oranges and browns and linger there a minute longer.

Let us spend our narrowing day taking in the world through the lens of Van Gogh with every leaf and desiccated stem a brush stroke of brilliance on the canvas of dusk.

Let us be transfixed by their beauty and may our gaze be shown mercy in the brilliance of the sun and autumn winds.

Let us be beholden to the blessing that is the world and this world beholden to this moment of blessing.

Let us for this one moment know that beauty is defined and existence, as short as it may be, is meant to be admired.

Rise

Only when we fall can we rise.

Only when we have suffered can we be healed.

Only when we have been truly broken can we then be truly fixed.

Only when we have tasted defeat can we truly appreciate victory.

Let us rise and fight beside each other.

Let us rise and struggle and toil, hand in hand.

Let us rise and love fiercely together.

Let us rise and be vulnerable, fearing neither the blade of steel nor of words.

Regardless of who we are, where there is darkness, seek the light.

Regardless of where we've been, where there is darkness, embrace the light.

Regardless of when it all happened, when there is darkness everywhere, be the light.

We are travelers here, away from home,

With a chance to prove each and every day that we draw life,

That darkness cannot prevail,

That goodness is not a theory,

And that meaning pursued is truth lived.

Go forth.

Go and shatter the shackles of fear

And rise, rise,

RISE.

A Multiple-Choice Monday

7:55 am on my Monday day off, the doorbell buzzed
again and again, rattling me out of my bed on a frigid
winter day. It's my day off and I wanted so badly to
sleep in after a very late last night. It was my neighbor
who locked himself out of his home and needed his spare
key.

Cold and groggy, my forty something year old body
couldn't fall back asleep afterwards. Mid-life insomnia at
its finest.

By the time 9:40 am hits, I could feel my fist eager to rise
up and shake towards heaven. The slumber that is owed
to me has been denied.

But no. It's better to get up and push through. Angry as I
am. Grumpy as I am. Tired as I am. Life must continue.

The world turns on its unyielding axis.

And as much as I want to flip over the game board and
start over, rearranging its pieces back in place, what is a
man's life but a vapor in the wind?

I will make this moment important. The coffee that I
brew now, I will make it matter.

In my being, I wrote down a multiple-choice quiz.

> Shall I spend today:
>   a. Whining
>   b. Wallowing in victimhood
>   c. In passive aggressive blaming
>   d. None of the above and why?

I stare at my coffee, its therapeutic aroma reminding me that all can still be well. With a steady sip, I select my answer wisely.

I choose 'd', because I know I could do better than all of the above.

We All Matter

Written 12/4/21

It's December 4, 2021 at the time I'm writing this. The new COVID variant, the Omicron variant, has shown up in the US within the past week. It appears to have originated in South Africa and, currently, very little is known about it.

At this point, I've come to accept that there will always be new variants of COVID and this will be the new normal in the near and likely distant future. One can only hope that with each new variant, humanity will get into the rhythm of preparing itself until the next one comes. Human existence in light of COVID has become a war of attrition.

Life continues on and the greater issues lie in how we respond to all of this, whether this has any effect on our individual purpose and on how we see ourselves. It goes without saying that as humans we are far from invincible. This has always been the case since the beginning of history. But despite our weakness, despite our vulnerabilities, does it make us less valuable in the grand scheme of things? I believe not.

Every individual has intrinsic value. Even though there are billions of us on the face of this earth; even though our lifespan is measured as a blink in the history of time, each person matters. We falter in making the mistake that the value of an individual can only be measured by their achievements, by their job title, or even by their monetary worth. In the end, when all is said and done, what good are these things when our time on this planet must leave with the fading twilight of life? Such a thought is too morbid, you may ask. Well, it's not so much morbid as it is true.

But what I mean to get at is this: we are unique creatures who are much more valuable than the money we can earn or the trophies we may accumulate. We dream. We invent and create. We often seek things, crave things, beyond our survival. We naturally have a grasp of what's right and wrong, though at times we may confuse and question ourselves. We do things, express things, are capable of things far more than any creature on this planet or possibly even the universe. Who are we to say that we are not special when so much evidence points to otherwise?

All that I've mentioned above is one of the reasons why I believe that we were designed, that we were created with intention for a greater purpose, by a greater being. Yes, I know some will be skeptical of this or have questions and such. I understand. It's a relevant struggle.

But to whoever may read this, I urge you to consider that perhaps we are more than just our physical bodies, that the universe is far more immense and far greater in possibility than what's in front of us each and every day. Or even consider that there may be greater things that happen in front of us each and every day and we must bring ourselves to notice them more. I believe in both.

I believe in love and that it's more than just an evolved survival instinct or a chemical reaction in the gelatinous organ we call a brain. I believe that God is love. I also believe in evil and the absence of love in this world that we call home. And I also believe that even though God is love, He values free will too.

Omicron variant or not, racial conflicts or not, international wars or not, we are challenged each and every day to question whether the choices that we make matter in light of the bigger picture. We are challenged each day to ask whether *we* actually matter. Reader, I leave these questions to you. But as for me I will make my answer known. The choices that we make do matter and we, including each and every single person on this earth, actually matter. Earthly achievements or not, impressive job title or not, and money in the bank or not; we all matter.

Reference Points

Hallgrímskirkja church (2019)

Reference Points

Cairns 1 (2019)

Cairns 2 (2019)

A Study of Light and Darkness

Photo by Austin Tam (2021)

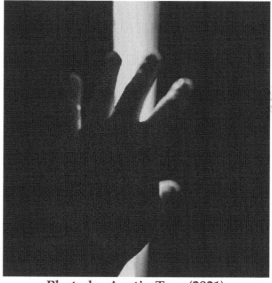

Photo by Austin Tam (2021)

A Study of Light and Darkness

Photo by Austin Tam (2021)